CHANGING YOUR
GAME

CHANGING YOUR
GAME

A Man's Guide
to Success with Women

Christie Hartman, PhD

5280
PRESS

Published by
5280 Press, LLC
PO Box 12477, Denver, CO 80212
www.5280Press.com

ISBN 10: 0984826211
ISBN 13: 978-0-9848262-1-6

Printed in the United States of America

This publication is designed to provide accurate and authoritative information with regard to the subject matter covered. It is sold with the
understanding that the publisher is not engaged in rendering legal,
accounting, or other professional advice. If legal advice or other expert
assistance is required, the services of a competent professional person
should be sought.

– From a *Declaration of Principles* jointly adopted by
a Committee of the American Bar Association and a
Committee of Publishers and Associations

Production and cover design by Chris Voeller

CONTENTS

WHY I WROTE THIS BOOK

I wrote this book for many reasons. The primary reason is that numerous men asked me to. "You have all these books for women," they pointed out, "but what about us?" Men too find dating challenging and want to learn the tools to succeed at it.

If men want to understand women better or improve their dating success, they don't have many resources to choose from. Of the dating advice books written for men, most are aimed at trolling bars to get women into the sack, and few to none are written by experts on human behavior.

That's where I come in.

Changing Your Game is about achieving success with women. What is success, you ask? Success is *getting what you want most*. Whether you're looking for a one-nighter, dates, a girlfriend, or a wife, the underlying principles behind dating success are the same. The truth is, men who succeed with women differ from men who don't. Sure, some of these men may have a repertoire of techniques or tactics they employ, but the rest of them have something much more important – the right *mindset*. These men think about dating and women in an entirely different way. You too can learn this mindset and achieve the success you want with women. You too can change your game.

What This Book Offers You

Changing Your Game offers several things. First, being a psychologist and scientist, most of what I preach is strongly research-based. This means that I base my advice on scientific research findings, established psychological principles, and research I've conducted through reading, observation, coaching, and countless interviews with men and women.

Second, this book provides tons of advice, but it also offers you a peek into the fascinating psychology behind dating and women. Sure, you can follow an expert's advice, but if you understand the principles behind it, you will be far ahead of most men.

Third, this book gives you detailed advice on such 21st century dating challenges as dating online, dating older women, and dating single moms. Times have changed, and the usual advice on how to pick up women in bars won't fly.

Finally, I provide a woman's point of view. While I think it's important for you to seek advice from male experts, real success in dating means learning to see things from a woman's standpoint. After all, women are your target market. The more you know about women, and the more you understand women, the more you'll succeed with women. It's that simple.

As you already know, dating can be filled with challenges. You can let those challenges thwart your success with women; or, you can let me show you how to tackle them head on.

Enjoy.

MINDSET:
THE FOUNDATION OF
DATING SUCCESS

1) THE #1 PREDICTOR OF SUCCESS WITH WOMEN

When you think about the traits that women like in men, what comes to mind? In other words, which traits lead to success with women? If you're like most men, you might guess that men who succeed with women have good looks, a successful career, money, confidence, charm, or even a great sense of humor. However, while all those traits can help you succeed with women, there is one crucially important factor that supersedes them all, that determines whether you'll be the guy with a great woman in your life or the guy who spends his life pissing and moaning about women. What is that all-important factor?

It's your attitude.

What is attitude? Your attitude reflects your general outlook about dating, women, and love. Is your attitude generally positive, in that you enjoy women and believe you can get what you're looking for? Or is it somewhat negative, where you don't trust women and doubt that the right one is out there?

Succeeding with women requires building a strong foundation upon which to develop dating skills. A positive attitude about dating and women is the first and *most important* pillar of this foundation. A good attitude will, over time, bring you success with women. A bad attitude will do the opposite. I have a saying: Attitude determines your success before you ever go out on a date.

Attitude determines your success before you ever go out on a date.

A bad attitude can be a sneaky and insidious, to the point where a man may not even realize his attitude needs work. The following are some quotes I've heard from men:

Bad Attitude about Dating

"Dating sucks – it's awkward and unnatural."

"I met a bunch of flakes online and refuse to try it again."

"All the good women have boyfriends and there's nothing left for me."

"Women have all the power in dating."

Bad Attitude about Women

"In my experience, women mainly care about how much money you make."

"Women need to stop being so self-entitled and expecting everything to be provided for them."

"Women use sex to manipulate men and get what they want."

"Beautiful women are spoiled and used to getting everything they want."

Bad Attitude about Yourself

"I'm short and women only want tall guys."

"I lost my hair – women don't like balding guys."

"Rich and successful men can get any women they want."

"Women don't want to date a loser like me."

Every one of these quotes signifies a bad attitude. If you can relate to one or more of the above statements, your attitude could use some work.

Dating and relationships mean that, from time to time, you will get hurt. And no matter how bad your experiences have been, it's your attitude about these experiences that's holding you back, not the experiences themselves. And while it's natural to feel some negativity after a bad date (or ten bad dates), this should be temporary. If it lingers, your bad attitude will drive your dating life right over a cliff.

What Causes a Bad Attitude?

Many things can contribute to a bad attitude, but typically it comes from having one or more negative experiences. Out of fear of repeating those bad experiences, we may cultivate a negative or cynical attitude and use it as a shield, hoping it will protect us. Some people hold on to this "shield" too long, until it becomes a part of them. When this happens, you don't control your attitude; it controls you.

Most people, male or female, believe their attitudes about the other sex are based on reality. However, most of the time, "reality" isn't reality at all; it's the reality we've chosen to believe. And nine times out of ten, people who say they're "just being realistic" are actually being negative. Moreover, numerous research studies have shown that when people believe something, no matter how negative or absurd, they will automatically notice anything that confirms their belief and disregard anything that doesn't.[1]

For example, if a guy believes that all women are manipulative, he will remember every time a woman manipulated him, remember all stories from other men who've been manipulated, even write blogs about manipulative women, generating more comments from men who've also been manipulated. He won't notice women who don't behave this way. If he's really stubborn, he will tell the guy who claims his girlfriend isn't manipulative that he's a fool who refuses to see the truth. And a guy like this will scare away any decent woman and wind up alone.

Why Attitude is So Important

Your attitude matters because it determines the mentality you have when you approach or deal with women. When you have an interview for a job you really want, do you go into the interview thinking, "This company sucks. They probably won't appreciate me or what I have to offer." Probably not. And why not? Because you know that a negative attitude may come across to your interviewers, and lowers your chances of getting the job.

It's no different with women. Women can sense your attitude toward them. This means that a bad attitude will scare good women away and attract the very women you hope to avoid.

Often, people who have negative attitudes say, "Hey, I have a right to be negative. I've had a lot of bad experiences." Yes, studies have shown that negative experiences can sour one's attitude. However, just as many studies have shown that the opposite is true as well: a sour attitude can create negative experiences.

A sour attitude can create more negative experiences.

As I mentioned in the previous section, a bad attitude is often a shield against getting hurt again; unfortunately, it will usually have the opposite effect. If you've been hurt or disappointed, I will talk about how to deal with that in the next chapter.

What's interesting is that, if you look carefully, you'll find that a bad attitude is usually based on half-truth or even fallacy, not fact. The following examples illustrate what I mean:

> *"I met a bunch of flakes online and refuse to try it again."*
> Yes, there are flakes online, and losers and crazies too. But there are also plenty of good people like you, looking for the same thing you are. The trick is to learn the signs that a woman is a flake, and keep trying.

"All the good women have boyfriends and there's nothing left for me." If you haven't met any good single women lately, you need to emerge from your cave and look in new places. They're out there.

"Women have all the power in dating." Hey, remember that time you took a woman out and then never called her? Who had the power then? You have the power to call, to not call, or to walk away if a woman isn't good to you.

"Women use sex to manipulate men and get what they want." It takes two to tango. If a woman has power over you because she's hot or because you wanted sex, it's because *you* let her have it.

"Beautiful women are spoiled and used to getting everything they want." Some are, most aren't. Most beautiful women are just people who want to be liked for who they are, rather than used for their looks.

"My ex cheated on me and now I don't trust women." Most women are capable of being faithful.

"I'm short and women only want tall guys." Women like tall, but few *require* tall. I know many, many short men who are very successful with women.

"Rich and successful men can get any women they want." They wish. No man can get any woman he wants. Rich, successful men also attract women they *don't* want: gold-diggers and other undesirables.

As you can see, most of the time, a bad attitude isn't all that realistic. It's simply choosing to ignore the good and focus on the bad.

The Perils of Dating Advice

Ironically, sometimes dating advice, which is supposed to help you, can reinforce a crappy attitude. I've seen dating books for women that talk about men like they're all players, easily bored cheats, or jerks that women need to develop mad manipulation skills to handle. Likewise, some dating advice for men teaches men that women are capricious, care only about money, or will have you by the balls if you let them. These experts, female or male, have lousy attitudes, and then they teach them to others. These books aren't the solution; they're part of the problem.

No matter how you've been burned, don't fall into the trap of trusting anyone who advocates a mistrust of the other sex. The goal is always to *understand* the other sex. That's the only way to succeed.

Never trust any expert who advocates a mistrust of the other sex.

Cultivating a Good Attitude

When it comes to dating and women, there are two kinds of attitudes, and thus two kinds of men. It's important to remember them, because they provide the foundation for the rest of this book. These two types of men are:

1) Problem Solvers

2) Complainers

When faced with a problem or challenge in dating, you can focus on the problem or you can focus on the solution. Problem Solvers focus on finding solutions; they generally have better attitudes and more success with women. Complainers focus on problems; they often "give up" and spend more time complaining about dating or women than trying to fix the problem. Their dating lives stink because their attitudes stink.

The table below illustrates the mindset of a Complainer compared to that of a Problem Solver:

Complainer Mindset	Problem Solver Mindset
"I hate online dating. It's a waste of time."	"Online dating has not worked for me, so I will figure out what to do differently."
"Women are so self-entitled. They expect the man to provide everything."	"What's the story with these women I keep attracting, and what can I do to change it?"
"She said no to a date. Women are shallow and never give guys like me a chance."	"It sucks she said no. If I don't get a yes from the next girl, I'll figure out what I need to change so that I get a yes."
"I'm so fed up with dating. It's like one bad date after the next."	"I'm burned out. I think I'll take a break from dating and spend some time with the guys."

If you look at these two columns, notice that the Complainer blames something else for his unhappiness (e.g. online dating, women). Also notice that he takes a stance of powerlessness, like there's nothing he can do – this is because he's focused on the problem. In contrast, the Problem Solver, who also gets frustrated, doesn't waste time blaming – he focuses on finding a solution to the problem. Sure, he may get angry or vent to his friends, but then he launches into problem solving mode.

Dating will frustrate you at times. They key is what you choose to do about it. You can't control dating or women, but you can control how you handle them. This is what it means to have a good attitude. And your attitude is something you have 100% control over all the time.

You can't control dating or women, but you can always control how you handle them.

If you want to succeed with women, cultivate a Problem Solver's mindset. Start now. You'll be amazed at how much more powerful you'll feel when you stop focusing on what sucks and start focusing on what you can do, change, or learn.

You'll also find that a Problem Solver's mindset will serve you well in many areas of life beyond dating. For example, when you watch interviews with men who've become millionaires or otherwise succeeded in business, their stories aren't filled with one success after the next. Often, it's the opposite – they made mistakes, got burned, lost money, and failed, sometimes multiple times. It took years to succeed. The difference between them and other guys is they learned from their mistakes and kept trying. They were Problem Solvers at heart.

"What about Women's Attitudes toward Us?"

Can women also fall into the trap of the Complainer mindset about dating and men? Hell, yes! In fact, I devote an entire chapter about this topic in my dating book for women, *It's Not Him, It's YOU*. A crappy attitude will trash a woman's dating success just as fast as it will trash yours.

If you're like most men, you've dated a woman who didn't like or trust men, who insulted you or men in general. Think back to one of those times. How did it make you feel? Not good, right? You probably felt frustrated to be punished for the sins of men who came before you, and angry that you were being lumped in with those losers simply because you're a guy. You're a good guy – you want to be evaluated on your own merits. Well, so do women.

Just as it's your job to work on your attitude, it's women's job to do the same.

Any man can be a Problem Solver if he chooses. If you've been through a lot and your attitude has shifted toward the sour end of things, this chapter was probably difficult to read. No need to worry. A bad attitude can happen to any of us, and you have the power to change it any time you want. When you do, you'll be amazed at how much happier (and more successful with women) you'll be.

2) ARE YOU STUCK IN THE PAST?

The previous chapter discussed the harm that a bad attitude can do to your dating life. This chapter will discuss a major contributor to a bad attitude: past disappointment.

Dating, relationships, and marriage are filled with great things; but sometimes they can bring us pain. Serious pain. Sometimes, we hang on to that pain, loading it on our backs like a 500-pound pack, and lug it around everywhere we go for years. We then haul it onto our dates and into our new relationships in the form of emotional baggage. And that isn't good.

In laying the foundation for success for women, a good attitude is the first and most important pillar in that foundation; dealing with emotional baggage from the past is the second pillar. If you want to succeed with women, you have to dump this baggage; otherwise it will pollute your interactions with new women.

Lugging around emotional baggage from the past will pollute your interactions with new women.

Emotional baggage can come from many sources, but here are some common ones:

- Getting dumped by a woman you loved
- Being cheated on
- Getting cleaned out in a divorce
- Ending a relationship with a difficult woman
- Repeated lack of success in dating

Getting dumped by a woman you loved. Few things in life hurt more than having someone you love decide to move on. If there was ever a time when I've seen men cry, it's when this happens. Whether that relationship lasted three months or thirty years, it's difficult to put your time, effort, and resources into a woman, just to have her walk away.

However, as much as this hurts, it's important to remember that things always happen for a reason. If the woman who left did so because you didn't treat her right, consider that a powerful lesson learned. If you did treat her right but she still left, acknowledge that she wasn't the right girl for you. The right girl is still out there, looking for you, and she will stick around for the long haul.

Being cheated on. Finding out the woman you love (and trust) is sleeping with someone else is a horrible feeling. It cuts to the bone. It makes you doubt everything: her, women, yourself, relationships, even your ability to please a woman.

However, people cheat for one of two reasons: 1) they're not getting their needs met in the relationship and attempt to seek it elsewhere, or 2) they lack the ability to be monogamous at that time. Of course, cheating doesn't solve either problem, and it is never acceptable. Unfortunately, many people learn this lesson the hard way. As with getting dumped, you have to view infidelity as an opportunity to see what you could have done differently, and accept that your partner made a bad choice. That choice reflects who she is, not who you are. There are plenty of women who will appreciate a faithful man like you, and never cheat.

Getting cleaned out in a divorce. Divorce is devastating. It's devastating emotionally, financially, and logistically. A divorce can rob a man of his money, his home, his business, even his kids. And while divorce law is getting better about recognizing men's rights, not all divorce courts are created equally. And even when a divorce settlement is fair, a divorce can make a man feel like a big failure.

But you aren't a failure. You're a human being who did his best to make a marriage work, and it didn't last. And you're far from alone. The good thing about divorce is that it gives you an opportunity to begin again, start a new life, and eventually find a woman who fits well with who you are today.

Ending a relationship with a difficult woman. I have met way too many guys who've endured a few months (or years) with a difficult woman. Maybe she had bipolar disorder, an addiction, or a propensity to throw heavy objects at you. Or maybe she was one of those women who could not be happy, even if her life depended on it. This can take a toll on a guy's ability to trust women or relationships if he chooses to generalize this experience to all women.

Don't give up hope if you've been in this situation. Women with psychological problems are far less common than normal, healthy women. And if she was merely "difficult," she may need to grow up a little, or you and she were just incompatible. Remember: if you never picked the wrong girls, you wouldn't learn to appreciate the right ones.

Repeated lack of success in dating. There's nothing more frustrating than dating for five, ten, or twenty years, looking for the right girl, and not finding her. You feel like you keep striking out with women, like you can't seem to find the right one, or maybe that women don't seem to appreciate the guy you are. Unlike some of your friends, maybe you actually want to get married and have kids… but you can't find a woman to do it with! Or, maybe you aren't worried about marriage, and would like to find a woman who isn't worried about it either.

Don't despair. The only men who wind up bachelors forever are men who *choose* to be. You've heard the famous quote: "The definition of insanity is doing the same thing over and over, and expecting different results." Whatever you're doing, it isn't working. With some work, including reading this book, you can figure out what needs to change.

Signs That You're Stuck in the Past

Here are a few signs that you're still lugging around the 500-pound pack of your past:

You talk about your ex. People talk about what's most important to them. If you talk about your ex, that means she's still playing a pretty big role in your life. This is especially true if you talk about your ex while on a date. And if you badmouth your ex, you might as well wear a big flashing neon sign that says, "My ex really hurt me and I haven't gotten over it yet!" Is that what you want to convey to women? I didn't think so.

Most of the time, badmouthing your ex reflects badly on you, not her. It shows that you've chosen a Complainer's mindset. The Problem Solver refuses to badmouth his ex; his attitude is, "Hey, I'm not happy about what happened with my ex, but I'm going to learn from it and move on." Be the guy who learns from it and moves on. So much sexier.

This doesn't mean you have to like your ex, or think that what she did is okay. It means you choose to let go of the past. This also doesn't mean you can never talk about your ex. It means you choose an appropriate time to pull out the Ex Files for the purpose of moving on or sharing about your past with a new woman.

You're pissed off. I know a guy who refers to his ex as "What's-her-name." I know another guy whose lip curls anytime his ex is mentioned. If your blood boils or your stomach curdles at the site of your ex or even the mere thought of her, or if you're still annoyed about how things went down in the past, you're still lugging the past around with you. Problem Solvers get pissed off too, but only temporarily.

You refuse to talk about the past. I'm not a fan of rehashing the past. But an obstinate refusal to discuss the past is a surefire sign that you're still hauling it around with you. Instead of showing everyone your 500-pound pack, you pretend it isn't there. Sometimes it's good to talk about past pain to get rid of it or to let a trusted person know what you've been through.

You overreact. When you're hanging on to the past, you will overreact to things that remind you of it. For example, your ex cheated on you and now you think all flirty women or women in short skirts are sluts. Generally, men who don't trust women or hate women who remind them of their exes are still lugging the 500-pound pack around.

Your friends are tired of hearing about it. If your friends tell you, "Dude, you need to get over her," or roll their eyes when you mention a past relationship that went sour, they're telling you to remove the 500-pound pack and let the past go.

If you suffered through a recent breakup or other dating-related injury, a certain amount of talking about the ex, or envisioning her driving off a bridge, is normal. These are signs of grief. However, once a few months have passed, and certainly after a year, the above signs mean you're hauling around the past everywhere you go, letting it negatively influence all that happens with new women. If you want to succeed with women, it's time to dump it. The next section will show you how.

How to Dump the 500-Pound Pack

If you, like many men, notice that you're hanging on to some emotional baggage from the past, you can do something about it. Here are some suggestions for letting go of the past:

Grief is good. No matter how big or small your past hurt is, you cannot skip the grieving process. I've seen men try this, and it never works. These men wind up hanging on to their emotional baggage forever and it takes a toll on their future with women.

Grief isn't just about crying. It's about letting yourself feel pissed off, sad, depressed, hopeless, fearful, and apathetic after going through something difficult. If these feelings arise, just feel them. Don't act on the feelings and don't become mired in them. Just acknowledge the feeling until it fades. Eventually, it will fade completely. If you're open to it, talk to a therapist. I know men who have and it really helped them.

Figure out what you learned. A great Problem Solver's trick to make the most of a bad experience is to learn something from it. Each date that went nowhere, each rejection, and each past relationship teaches us something useful. Sometimes, it's as simple as, "I'm not her type." Other times it's, "Looking back, it makes sense that she cheated; after all, she flirted with every guy she saw!" or, "I loved her, but we never saw eye to eye on much of anything and, looking back, we weren't compatible."

Besides, if your ex didn't treat you like crap, how would you learn that you deserve more? If you and your ex hadn't fought like banshees, how would you learn to appreciate a woman you get along well with? As much as it sucks, we learn more from pain than we do from pleasure, so make the most of it.

We learn more from pain than we do from pleasure.

What you can do differently next time. Similar to figuring out what you learned from your rejections or breakups, a Problem Solver identifies what he can do differently next time. One man, after a terrible marriage to a mean woman, decided that next time he would choose a woman who was kind and more compatible with him. Another man, after getting rejected over and over, realized he was wasting his energy on women who weren't showing strong signs of interest, and tightened his standards.

Sometimes, if your situation was a bad one, it helps to sit and write down all that went wrong, in detail, followed by every single thing you would do differently if you had a chance to do it over. This exercise can be surprisingly helpful for letting go of the pain of what happened, and for ensuring you'll do the better thing next time.

Earn back that trust. Sometimes, after a painful breakup or event, men will say that they no longer trust women. However, you won't succeed with women if you don't trust them on a basic level. Moreover, apart from choosing the best women you can find, you can never guarantee that a woman won't hurt or betray you.

Often, when men say they don't trust women, what they really don't trust is their own ability to pick a good woman or to handle it when things don't work out. However, picking good women and handling loss are skills you learn from experience. All good things in life involve risk. If a relationship doesn't work, you can still choose to trust that, no matter what, you *will* handle it.

A lack of trust in women is really a lack of trust in yourself.

Success with women means letting go of the emotional crud you carry around from the past. Yes, dating and relationships mean getting hurt from time to time. Men with Problem Solver mindsets face the pain, figure out what went wrong, learn from it, and put the past behind them. They don't allow anger or bitterness from the past to ruin their futures. There's an old saying:

"Resentment is like drinking poison and hoping the other person will die."

If you've experienced disappointment, it's okay to feel angry or hurt. It's okay to avoid women for a while. Just make sure that phase is temporary. Then, choose to let it go and move on.

3) WHY ARE YOU DATING ANYWAY?

Successful people know what they want. This is true in dating, just as it's true in other areas of life. For example, people who achieve wealth know, from the very beginning, that they want to get rich. Gold medal winning athletes know, without a doubt, from the moment their training begins, that they want to win gold. Likewise, men who succeed with women know exactly what they want from them. Psychologically, being clear about your goals goes a long way in ensuring you will reach them.

Why is this? When you make a goal and stick to it, your mind unconsciously changes its focus – it begins to notice opportunities that will help you achieve your goal and ignore opportunities that will not. The solid foundation necessary to succeed with women has four pillars: you've learned the first two. The third pillar is knowing what you want out of dating.

When you venture into the world of dating, it's important to know what your purpose is. The clearer you are on what you want out of dating, the more likely you are to get it. This may sound obvious, but you'd be surprised at how many men date or get online without having thought much about why they're there. They know they want "companionship," but companionship comes in many packages. And if that package doesn't align with your goal, you will not succeed.

Four Types of Relationships

No matter what your age or situation, you date because you want one of four types of relationships:

1) **No strings attached (NSA).** This includes a one-nighter, a fling, or some other interaction that is sexually-based and short-term.

2) **Casual dating.** Here, you want more than sex. You want to date women, take them out, get to know them, and enjoy yourself, but you aren't looking to settle down with any one woman.

3) **Relationship.** This is when you want a girlfriend, a woman you have an exclusive relationship with, where you both only date each other.

4) **Marriage.** You're looking to legalize your relationship and spend the rest of your life with one special woman. Perhaps you are also looking to start a family.

Knowing which of these four types of relationships you want will steer you towards women who want the same as you, and prevent you from wasting your time and energy with women who can't give you what you want.

Here are a few ways that being unclear about what you want can get you into trouble:

Getting involved without considering if you both want the same thing. Single people focus on finding someone they feel mutual attraction with and who has the basic traits they're looking for. Rarely do they consider whether both parties want the same kind of relationship.

For example, you meet a woman you like, the chemistry is great and the sex even better, and then you find out she's hoping to marry and have kids, and you aren't really into that. Or, you meet an interesting woman online, things go great, and you fall ass over teakettle for her, and then she says she still wants to see other people because she just got divorced.

Why do we do this? Because we often automatically assume others want what we want. You might believe, "Hey, I met her at a *bar*; she can't possibly expect this to turn into a relationship!" or, "I thought all women wanted to get married!" It isn't until we meet someone who wants something radically different from us that we begin to consider how important this is!

You don't know what you want. Some men don't seek out the kind of relationship they want because they don't know what they want. This is more common in younger men, men who've been through a recent breakup or divorce, and men with commitment fears. To some extent, that's normal.

However, in my experience, most men in this category actually *do* know what they want, but for some reason they aren't comfortable admitting it to themselves. A common example is when a man wants NSA – he's afraid to admit it because he believes women will think he's a pig or because he was raised to believe that NSA is wrong. Another example is when a man, deep down, wants a relationship with one special woman, but after years of being the player is afraid of losing his edge and becoming "pussy-whipped." In other words, some men aren't entirely comfortable with what they really want.

Saying one thing, doing another. Many women have complained to me that a man said he wanted one thing, but then behaved otherwise. For example, a man says he wants a relationship, but then calls a woman infrequently and refuses to be called "boyfriend" after a couple of months. Likewise, a man says he wants something casual, then calls a woman every day and gets angry when he sees her with another man.

These men aren't clear about what they want. And, as a result, they bring drama into their lives.

You know what you want, but settle for something else because it's available. Sometimes, you know exactly what you want, you haven't found it yet, and this other situation is sitting right in front of you, tempting you. For example, you really want a relationship, but accept NSA because an NSA situation becomes available to you. Or, you like a woman and want to date her while seeing other women too, but you see only her because you know she'll freak out if you do otherwise.

Hey, I get it. You know you need to eat a good meal, but the waitress accidently dropped a chocolate brownie sundae in front of you. What's a man to do?

It can be hard to turn down something good in the hopes of finding something great. But if you don't, you avoid getting what you really want. What's worse is if you settle for the wrong thing, the wrong thing can linger for months, even years. Meanwhile, what you really want is still out there, and you're preventing yourself from getting it.

Here is an example of this. And like all examples in this book, it is from real life.

Example

Jason worked as a photographer in a major city. Due to his job, he was exposed to models and other Beauties on a regular basis. He'd done his share of playing and had been with many of these women. And, like many men in his position, he grew tired of it. He realized he was ready for a relationship.

Jason, at the advice of a female friend, started looking for women he could have a relationship with. But old habits are hard to break, and when a beautiful model came on to him, he went for it. They dated casually for a while, but it was mostly about the sex. Jason grew bored, and wondered why he couldn't find a relationship.

This is a classic example of taking the brownie sundae instead of holding out for the whole meal. Jason's problem does have a solution, and that's what I discuss in the next section.

How to Avoid Drama

As I've said, being unclear about what you want won't get you what you want. And, let's face it: not getting what you want sucks. Just as importantly, getting involved in a relationship that isn't what you want brings drama into your life. And I know you don't want drama.

This section provides pointers on how to identify what you want, stay focused on it, and avoid drama.

Get Clear

Task #1 is to get clear on what you want. Here are a few suggestions to help you gain that clarity:

1) Ask yourself, "If I knew what I wanted, it would be _____." The hypothetical can be surprisingly effective in getting to the truth.

2) Ask yourself, "If I knew that my friends, family, and women would be 100% supportive of it, what would I want?" Disapproval or retaliation from others is an extremely powerful factor that prevents you from going after what you want.

3) Once you figure out what you want, admit it out loud. Tell your friends. Write it on your bathroom mirror if you have to. This makes your intentions clearer.

Also, being clear on what you want means you can't want two things at the same time. In the earlier example, Jason wanted a relationship, but settled for NSA/casual dating because it was available to him. The NSA was nice, but it wasn't what he really wanted, it didn't make him happy, and it distracted him from his goal.

Pursuing multiple relationship goals also sends mixed messages to women, even if you don't intend to. You then risk attracting the wrong women and getting involved with them.

If you find you are torn between two things, choose the less involved one. For example, if torn between casual dating and a relationship, choose casual dating. This causes fewer problems, and you can always upgrade later, when you're ready.

Stay Clear

Knowing what you want is half the battle. However, as with any goal, it's easy to get sidetracked or to lose focus. To get what you want, you have to avoid things that pull you off track.

One thing that will pull you off track is changing what you want depending on the girl. In other words, to say, "Girl #1 is good for NSA, but Girl #2 is girlfriend material," is being unclear. As with the guy who wants two things, you send mixed messages to women, bring more problems upon yourself, and avoid getting what you truly want. Besides, how would you like it if a woman you really liked only considered you "casual dating guy" – a guy who will buy her dinner – while some other guy is worthy of her heart? You wouldn't.

Another thing that can pull you off track is when you get confused about what you want *now* versus what you want in the future. If you meet a woman you really like who wants marriage and kids, knowing you want those things "someday" isn't the same as wanting them. "Someday" is useless. You either want to get married or you don't. And if you don't – if you only want a relationship – there's nothing wrong with that.

Finally, pressure from women, judgment from others, or a need for companionship can dissuade you from seeking what you want. Don't let that happen. Any of the four types of relationships are completely legitimate. Often, when people give you a hard time about something you want, it's because they sense that you aren't completely comfortable with it. If you're clear and confident, people will back off.

If you aren't comfortable with what you want, people will hassle you about it.

Find Out What She Wants

Being clear helps attract women who want what you do. But you also have to find out what she wants. True, it isn't appropriate in most situations to ask a woman right off the bat what she's looking for. Thus, until you've gotten to know her a bit, you have to do some sleuthing. Some women state outright what they're looking for (or *not* looking for). Otherwise, pay attention to her commentary about dating or relationships. Is she just getting back into dating again after a divorce? Is she hoping to have kids? Does she complain that too many men want to get too serious? Each of these hints gives you some information. Eventually, after a few dates, just ask her.

However, women too can be conflicted about what they want – for example, a woman who goes home with you after you met her in a bar (which indicates an interest in NSA) may want to keep seeing you (which indicates a desire for dating or a relationship). So you'll have to pay close attention.

Finding out what she wants also means respecting what she wants. Never try to talk a woman out of what she wants because it isn't what you want. For example, if you're looking for casual dating and a woman wants you to stop seeing other women or to meet her parents, don't say, "Why are you being so serious? Just relax and have fun." This is trying to convince her to want what you want. Instead, say you aren't looking to be exclusive and don't feel comfortable meeting the folks. Likewise, don't pretend to want what she does to keep her around. This is dishonest, and you'll both waste years in something that goes nowhere and ends badly.

If You Change Your Mind, Say So

Sometimes, a man will change his mind. He will get involved with a woman thinking he wants a relationship, and then realize he isn't ready for one. Or, he'll meet a woman for NSA or casual dating, then wind up falling for her. Often, this is due to being unclear, but sometimes a man realizes that what he wants has changed for good.

If this happens, speak up. Get clear on what you want, then tell her you thought you were ready for X, but are really looking for Y. She'll either be game, or she won't.

Let Go of the Wrong Women

Knowing what you want means letting go of anything that doesn't fit the bill. It means staying on task and turning down the brownie sundae so you can have a gourmet meal. I know it's tough to walk away from someone you like, from regular sex or companionship. It's very easy to make excuses or rationalize staying in a situation that's "better than nothing." We've all done it at one time or another. But settling for Ms. Wrong or lingering in a lopsided relationship won't bring you success. And isn't that the whole point, to succeed with women?

"What if I'm Horny as Hell?"

Let's face it: the longer you've been single (and celibate), the harder it is to avoid getting into relationships that aren't what you want. It becomes much easier to justify dating the wrong people, to the point where you will even deceive yourself!

Some friends and I recently discussed how long you have to go without before your standards begin to sink. For some, it's a month or two; for others, six months or a year. If you haven't gotten some lovin' in a while, you too will have a period of time after which your standards go south. The best way to deal with this challenge is to be aware of it. Awareness won't guarantee you'll make the right decisions, but it increases your odds of doing so. Once you realize you're not getting what you want, make your (polite) exit and keeping looking.

No matter what happens in the crazy adventure we call dating, always know why you're dating. Know what your goal is. It may change over time, and that's okay. When you keep your eyes on your goal, what you want will come to you.

4) STANDARDS: LOOKING FOR THE RIGHT WOMEN

When you're at a party and talking to women, or browsing on an online dating site, you probably have some idea of what kind of women you like. You have certain traits you want, whether physical or otherwise, and others you don't want. You may keep a mental list of these traits whenever you meet a woman, or perhaps you just "know it when you see it." Either way, there are certain traits you can live with, and other traits you can't. These are your dating standards.

The first four chapters of this book represent the four pillars of success with women. They provide the foundation upon which successful dating builds. The first pillar is a good attitude. The second pillar is freeing yourself from the past. The third is knowing exactly what you want out of dating. And the fourth pillar? Establishing good dating standards.

Before I launch into what good standards are, it's important to first understand what creates attraction. Why is this important? Because, to some extent, who you're attracted to reflects your dating standards.

Your attraction to a woman reflects your dating standards.

If you have good standards, you'll attract higher quality women and have greater success in dating. With poor standards, the opposite will occur.

What Makes You Attracted to a Woman?

Think about the last time you felt attracted to a woman. Perhaps you felt it with the fit woman you've seen at the gym but never met. Or maybe you're attracted to the girl who works in your company's marketing department, who you've chatted with for years but never dated. Or perhaps the last time you felt attraction was with the woman you spent four years in a relationship with, until things suddenly ended. Whoever it was, it's no coincidence that she interested you, while other women didn't.

The Two C's

So what causes attraction and interest? Interest and attraction are really about the two C's: chemistry and compatibility. When you're interested in a woman or find her attractive, you're experiencing chemistry, compatibility, or both.

Chemistry. Chemistry is when a woman "does it" for you. She looks good to you. You look at her. You want to talk to her. You wonder what it's like to have sex with her. You may feel nervous in her presence. You get that crazy, gaga feeling.

Chemistry can be physical, emotional, or intellectual. When you like a woman's looks and want to have sex with her, that's physical chemistry. However, good chemistry goes beyond the physical, such as when you find a woman interesting, enjoy talking with her, feel connected to her, and/or feel a desire to care for or protect her. She is special and stands out to you, more so than other women who may be just as good-looking (or more so).

It is not uncommon for men to feel physical chemistry for a woman before they feel emotional or intellectual chemistry. In other words, you may find her looks fascinating before you find her personality fascinating.

Men often feel physical chemistry for a woman before they feel emotional or intellectual chemistry.

Generally, chemistry is either there on some level, or it isn't. And there isn't much you can do to create it with someone. A lack of chemistry with a woman doesn't mean there's something wrong with her or that she isn't attractive; it just means she isn't for you. Likewise, if a woman feels no chemistry with you, she can't help that either. Also, while chemistry can be instant, it can also take time to develop.

Compatibility. Compatibility refers to how well-matched you are with a woman, or how well you and she fit together. It assesses whether what you want and need meshes with what she wants and needs. Unlike chemistry, compatibility doesn't hit you with that powerful, intoxicating feeling. However, compatibility is just as important as chemistry if you want your relationship to last, and is a crucial factor when setting your standards.

Compatibility is based on a series of different criteria, including, but not limited to:

1) **Appearance:** her looks and personal style

2) **Dating goals:** NSA, casual dating, relationship, marriage/kids

3) **Personality:** talkative, reserved, opinionated, funny, sweet, serious

4) **Lifestyle:** hobbies, how she spends her free time, drug/alcohol habits

5) **Profession:** her education, job, work habits

6) **Intellect:** brainy vs. down-to-earth, interest in reading and intellectual topics

7) **Baggage:** her marital history, kids, family and personal history

8) **Life goals:** plans for her life and future, whether she wants kids

9) **Values:** religious beliefs, political views, family values, gender roles, sexuality

The more compatible you are with a woman in the above areas, the more likely you and she will mesh, and the more success your relationship will have. Compatibility can range from nonexistent to great, with everything in-between. The more serious a relationship you want, the more compatibility you'll need and the more items you'll need to consider from the above list. For example, if you're looking for NSA, you will probably only need to consider items 1-2. If you're looking for a relationship, you'll need to venture beyond items 1 and 2. For marriage, you'll need to evaluate all nine items on the list.

It's important to note that good compatibility doesn't mean you and a woman are *the same* in all the above areas. It means that you and she need to *mesh* in these areas, either because you're similar or because any differences work for you. For example, with personality, talkative people are often compatible with quieter people because their styles complement one another, rather than clash with one another.

Typically, chemistry creates your initial attraction in a woman, but compatibility keeps you interested. Chemistry can be quick and powerful; compatibility is slower and more subtle. Have you ever met a woman you were fascinated with, and then suddenly lost interest in her after a few dates or after you had sex? Chances are there was chemistry, but little or no compatibility.

Chemistry gets you together; compatibility keeps you together.

Finally, as with chemistry, a lack of compatibility with a woman doesn't mean there's something wrong with her, or with you—it just means you aren't a good match.

Example

Joseph and Ally met at a party and hit it off immediately. They were both attractive, smart, and funny. They enjoyed each other's company, and started dating seriously. However, over time, they began to experience friction. Joseph loved to go out with his friends on the weekend, have a few drinks, even smoke weed now and again. He wasn't an addict, and was a responsible guy. However, Ally hated going out, rarely drank, and never smoked weed. She disapproved of Joseph's habits and felt that, at 34, he was too old to be doing such things.

You might think that Ally was uptight and judgmental of Joseph's lifestyle. Or, maybe you think that Joseph should grow up and stop partying at his age. Whatever your opinion, it is neither right nor wrong. Joseph and Ally were compatible in many areas, but lacked compatibility in their personalities and their lifestyles. Joseph was an outgoing, social guy who enjoyed partying and staying out late. Ally was a quieter, more health-conscious woman who preferred to stay home with Joseph. Neither was wrong; they just weren't a good match.

Standards: Putting the Two C's to Work for You

There is a lot of confusion over what it means to have "good" or "poor" standards when you date. Generally speaking, good standards means choosing a woman you experience the two C's with; poor standards means settling for a woman you don't feel the enough of the two C's with. In other words, you want good chemistry (all three types) mixed with strong compatibility. The more of each you have, the better you'll get along and the longer the relationship will last.

Having good standards means choosing a woman you experience the two C's with.

The following table provides some examples of good vs. poor standards:

Good Standards	Poor Standards
Waiting to see if you have something in common with a woman you're really attracted to.	Jumping in with both feet because she's the hottest woman you have ever seen.
"I want a woman I can talk to, who wants what I want out of life."	"As long as she's pretty and likes football, I'm cool."
Dating women you're attracted to.	Targeting 9s and 10s.
Being open to a variety of attractive women.	Only wanting younger women or blondes.
"I don't want a girlfriend right now. If she wants exclusivity, then I'm out."	"I don't want to be exclusive, but if I tell her that, she'll freak out or leave me."
Getting rid of women who don't show clear signs of interest.	Putting up with a woman's mixed messages or unreliable behavior because you like her.
Ditching women who don't treat you right.	Tolerating poor treatment because you love her or because she's hot.
Going without companionship or sex until you meet a woman you share the two C's with.	Taking what you can get because you're bored, lonely, or horny.

As I mentioned earlier, who we're attracted to reflects our standards. Thus, if you aren't succeeding with women, it's time to change your standards.

While anyone can have poor standards, men and women have different tendencies when it comes to this. Women tend to care a lot about compatibility, sometimes *too much*, to the point where some women have mile-long lists of traits they "must" have in a man. This is not good, and I devote a chapter to this in *It's Not Him, It's YOU*. Men, however, may worry less about compatibility and focus too much on physical chemistry. Why do you think beautiful women get so much attention?

While emphasizing chemistry over compatibility is fine if you know you want NSA, it's a mistake if you want anything more. Why is this? Chemistry is called "chemistry" for a reason – when we experience it, neurotransmitters flood our brains, especially in brain areas that involve reward. This is why you feel infatuated or nuts over a woman early on. But anyone who's been in a long term relationship knows that this neurotransmitter bath doesn't last, and when it wanes, there needs to be something else to maintain the attraction.

That "something else" is compatibility. Chemistry without compatibility causes a relationship to fizzle out quickly. Or, if the relationship manages to last, it will be rocky and miserable.

Without good compatibility, even the strongest of physical attractions will fizzle out.

Finally, chemistry doesn't have to be instant to be strong. We all love the idea of "love at first sight," and every man knows what "lust at first sight" feels like. Yes, this feels great, but it doesn't always happen that way. Many men have told me that they developed chemistry with a woman they weren't interested in initially, after becoming acquainted with her. If you meet a woman and don't feel physically attracted to her right away, but like her or find her interesting, don't rule her out yet.

When I was writing this book, a male friend of mine struggled with this chapter. He said he felt like I was telling men to "skip dessert and eat their spinach." I laughed at his example. But, no. No, no, no.

I don't want you to skip dessert. Skipping dessert sucks. Instead, I want you to *have it all* – the great meal AND the dessert. When you hold out for the two C's, you get the woman you think is beautiful AND who you get along great with. Chasing the rush of chemistry and ignoring compatibility is like eating dessert for every meal – it's bad for you and it eventually gets old.

Having good standards brings you better women and prevents drama, breakups, divorce, and other difficulties. The more you aim for women you're compatible with, the more your standards will rise, making it even easier to find the right women and weed out the wrong ones.

The first four chapters of this book are all about building a strong foundation. You've taken on a Problem Solver's attitude, dumped off your past baggage, gotten crystal clear about what you want, and now you've set your standards. You've done the lion's share of the work and you're miles ahead of most men.

You're ready.

SUCCESS
AND WOMEN

5) WOMEN APPROACH DATING DIFFERENTLY

Men and women are different. And while men and women date for much of the same reasons – to find someone who wants what they want – women often approach this goal differently than men do. Why is this? Because women are wired a bit differently then men, and socialized a bit differently than men. These differences are part of what attracts you to women. They're also what baffles you about them.

To succeed with women, it's important to understand their approach to dating and why they do the things they do. While the Complainer grumbles about women's dating tendencies or ignores them in the hopes that they'll go away, the Problem Solver faces them head on and seeks to understand them.

The next section discusses several ways that women approach dating differently than men. These rules don't apply to all women, all of the time. But they are general tendencies you will see in most women, so it's important to be aware of them.

Women Develop Physical Chemistry More Slowly

In Chapter 4, I said that men often feel physical chemistry for a woman before they feel chemistry or intellectual chemistry. In other words, you may be attracted to a woman and/or want to sleep with her before you really know much about her, before you develop other feelings for her. Again, this isn't true every time, but it's true more often than not.

This is not the case with women. Women often feel intellectual or emotional chemistry for a man *before* they feel physical chemistry. Alternatively, women can develop all three types of chemistry at once. In other words, a woman may find you interesting or like being around you before she feels physically attracted to you. For women, physical attraction is complex and may take time.

This simple difference creates all kinds of dating problems. For example, have you ever had a woman seem interested in you, laugh at your jokes, and tell you you're awesome, just to say no to a date or tell you she wants to be "just friends?" This confuses men. But it's very simple: this means she likes you (i.e. feels some type of intellectual or emotional chemistry) but feels no physically chemistry for you. You, on the other hand, are more likely to talk to a woman or find her interesting *because* you're physically attracted to her on some level. If you don't find her physically attractive, you probably won't even talk to her.

Here's another example: you go out on a date with a woman, things go well, and you wind up in bed with her. She calls you several times over the next few days, and is confused when you don't call back because you seemed interested and you had a great time together. You, on the other hand, have no interest in seeing her again. Why does this happen? Because women feel other forms of chemistry before or at the same time as they develop physical chemistry. If she has sex with you, she's physically attracted to you, which means she's probably already attracted to you in other ways and, therefore, interested in seeing where things go. But since men develop physical attraction first, you may have enjoyed the date and sex but never developed enough intellectual or emotional chemistry with her to pursue the relationship beyond that.

Women are very social and can genuinely like a guy they aren't attracted to. This is how a man winds up in the "Friend Zone." A Complainer takes this personally or gets mad about it. A Problem Solver knows that just as he can't help feeling no physical attraction to certain women, they can't help feeling no physical attraction him. And he moves on. However, if you get stuck in the Friend Zone often, you'll want to take more time reading Chapters 6 and 7.

Women Want Relationships or Marriage

As I discussed in Chapter 3, singles want one of four types of relationships when dating: No Strings Attached (NSA), casual dating, a relationship, or marriage. What a man wants will depend on his personality, his age, and where he is in his life; but at any given time, the average man can fall into any of these four categories with roughly equal probability.

Not the case with women. While many women are open to NSA or casual dating from time to time, they are much more likely to seek relationships or marriage. In other words, most women date to find a boyfriend or husband, not a screw buddy or a casual companion. Women date with a purpose, especially once they're over 25.

This too can create misunderstandings in dating. For example, a woman who has sex on the first date may appear to want NSA, but may actually want more. A more common example is when you're dating a woman and feel that things are going well, and then suddenly she wants to know "where things are going" or want to DTR (Define The Relationship). To you, it may seem like she's rushing things or getting too serious. But she's simply trying to find out if you want the same things she wants. If there's one thing women hate, it's wasting time and energy on men who don't want what they want.

Not all women who are looking for a relationship or marriage are desperate or trying to nail you down, no matter how determined they may seem. Women are relationship-oriented and they don't generally value relationships that don't have a purpose beyond momentary fun. They fear being used for sex or being strung along by men who say they want a future but then don't step up. While these things probably don't seem like a big deal to you – hell, you probably wouldn't mind being used for sex from time to time! – they're extremely unpleasant for women.

Where a Complainer might gripe that women are marriage-hungry or that they pressure him, a Problem Solver knows that just because a woman wants these things doesn't mean that he has to.

Women Think about the Future

When a woman meets a man or goes out on a date with him, no matter how independent she is or how slowly she wants to take things, in the back of her mind she is often thinking:

"Does this guy have future potential?"

"Is this man husband material?"

"Does he want a family?"

"Could he be The One?"

This is often the case even if a woman isn't looking for marriage, because she knows that any involvement can turn into something more. Some men do this too, especially when they're ready to settle down. But women do it far more, even with men they barely know. A wise woman knows not to take such thoughts too seriously. Otherwise, she may come across as getting too serious too soon, even if she isn't.

Example

Oliver (44) is divorced with two children, ages 10 and 12. He's actively dating, but has not thought much about the future. One day, I ran into Oliver and he told me he was frustrated with dating never-married women in their 30s. Why those women, I asked him? He would date one of these women, things would be going fine, and then suddenly she would ask the inevitable question: "Where are we?" This made Oliver feel pressured, and his response to me was, "I just thought we were having dinner."

What is the problem here? Oliver's dates were focused on where the relationship was going (i.e. the future), while he was focused on simply enjoying a meal with these women (i.e. the present). These women didn't want to waste time with a guy who didn't what want they wanted. And it's pretty clear what these women wanted: a never-married woman in her 30s is often looking to marry and have kids. By contrast, a divorced dad in his 40s, like Oliver, has already done all that and is just looking to enjoy himself. These women were not compatible for him.

Oliver was a Complainer who focused on the problem. A Problem Solver would have recognized these women didn't want what he wanted, and focused on finding women who did.

It can be startling when a woman brings up the future, especially when the only future you've thought about is whether she's sleeping at your house that night. When a woman does this, you may feel like she's desperate for marriage or trying to get too serious. This may be true in some cases, but more often she is simply trying to assess if you too are open to a potential future, or if she's wasting her time with a guy who, like Oliver, isn't concerned with future marriage or kids.

How to Handle the "Where Are We?" Conversation

Instead of reacting with fear or resistance when a woman brings up the future, a Problem Solver does the opposite: he's glad she brought it up. Why? One of the four pillars of success with women is knowing what you want. And if she wants to know "where things are," you get to find out what she wants. If she doesn't want what you do, you can send her packing.

Here are some questions you might hear from a woman who is thinking about the future:

"Where do you see this going?"

"What are you looking for?"

"Are you seeing other women?"

"Are we in a relationship?"

If you find yourself at the receiving end of these kinds of questions, ask her what she's looking for. Whatever answer she gives you, react neutrally. Remember: just because a woman wants to get married doesn't mean you have to marry her! You're free to choose whatever you want! Then, when it's your turn to state what you want, here are some suggestions on what to say:

If you aren't looking for a relationship or marriage, or know you aren't interested in a future with her, say:

"I like you, but I just want to enjoy dating. I'm not ready to be exclusive."

"I just got divorced and I'm not ready for a relationship."

"I like you, but I don't see us together long term."

"I like being with you, but I'm only interested in dating casually."

These statements are honest and clear without being hurtful. Notice that each clearly states what you want, or don't want. Also, these statements aren't vague. Being vague shows a lack of confidence. True, she may want to stop seeing you when she finds out the truth. So what? You have a goal, and you don't want to waste your time with women who impede that goal.

If you are interested in something long term, but haven't really thought about the future yet or aren't sure about her yet, say:

"I would like something long term, but I'm not ready to think about the future yet."

"I would like a family someday, but not for at least a few more years."

"I don't know what the future holds for us yet, but I'm willing to stick around and find out."

This establishes that you aren't thinking about the future yet but aren't necessarily opposed to one. The only women who will have a problem with this are ones who are really ready to marry or have kids right now, in which case you're not the guy for her.

If you know you're interested in a future with her, but don't feel ready for anything formal yet, say:

"I do see a potential future for us, but I don't want to rush into anything."

"I like/love you, and I want to see where this goes."

"I'm not seeing other women. I like being with you and want to see where it leads."

Overall, don't worry about giving her an answer she won't like. What *you* want matters just as much as what she wants, and it isn't your job to fulfill her wishes simply because she has them. Your only obligation is to know what you want and convey that to her.

Some women put too much pressure on men about the future. This often results from bad experiences: many women have wasted years with men who, for example, said they wanted marriage but then never stepped up to the plate. Other women seem desperate to marry, and don't seem to care about who they marry as long as they find a husband or someone to give her children. However, the average woman isn't like this. In the end, either you both want the same thing, or you don't.

If You Want to Understand Women...

If you want to understand women better – and put yourself at a huge advantage over other men – here are a few suggestions to try:

Hang out with women. Unless they were raised with lots of sisters, most men spend little time around other women until they get into relationships. And then they wonder why they find women so perplexing! Hang out with as many women as you can, including your mom, aunts, sisters, cousins, roommates, or coworkers. Go to lunch with them, have a beer with them, go to some yoga classes. This will teach you much and will also make you even more comfortable around women, which will pay off when you date.

Ask women's opinions. If you want to understand how women approach dating, ask them their opinions about dating topics. Ask them what they love (and don't love) about men. Different women will have different answers, but after a while you will begin to see patterns. You can also ask women's opinions about you – your appearance, your manners, or anything that might influence your success with women. You don't have to take the advice or even agree with their opinions. But listening to them will teach you a lot.

Read dating advice written for women. This is a secret trick that most men would never, ever try. Dating advice for women – and there is a LOT of it – is filled with revealing information about what women want from men, and what they struggle with. Men who've read the books I've written have told me they learned a lot about women.

I know this is a lot of information to absorb. Give it time to sink in. The more you understand the way women approach dating, the more success you'll have with them.

6) THE TESTOSTERONE EFFECT, PART ONE: WHAT ATTRACTS WOMEN?

If you Google anything about attracting women, you will get a very long list of websites claiming to know the secrets to doing so. Some of these websites are decent; many others are laughable, promising that in exchange for your hard-earned money they can give you the secrets to having droves of hot women begging you for sex.

If only it were that simple.

So what attracts women? Money? Sure. But there are plenty of guys making modest incomes who succeed with women.

Good looks? Okay. But what about all those average looking men who never seem to be without women? How do they do it?

Being an "alpha male?" Fine. But there are tons of males who have zero leadership skills and are about as alpha as a teddy bear, and women love them.

So what is it? What attracts women?

This question is really two questions:

1) What attracts women initially?

2) What keeps women interested?

A lot of dating advice for men focuses only on question #1. These advice-givers assume that attracting women means succeeding with them. They're wrong. After all, a beautiful woman will attract lots of men, but she won't necessarily keep them interested, especially if the only thing she has going for her is her looks.

Attracting women initially is a great start. But true success with women goes beyond that. This chapter will discuss the men who succeed with women, and what makes them special.

Attraction 101: What Attracts Women Initially?

Many, many scientific studies have examined male-female attraction and what attracts each sex to the other. If you want to know what attracts women to men initially, I can tell you in one word:

Testosterone.

Testosterone makes men masculine. Women are biologically attracted to the physical signs of testosterone, such as taller stature, greater muscularity, and deeper voice. Testosterone doesn't just affect men's physical appearance, either – exposure to high testosterone levels in the womb and once more at puberty influences men's brain development and behavior. This is why men may think or behave differently than women. And these differences are attractive to women.

This is no different than men finding big breasts, a round ass, full lips, or high heels attractive in women. These are all signs of estrogen, which gives women their femininity. It's no coincidence that Kim Kardashian, who exhibits all of these traits, is so popular among men. Men are attracted to estrogen and women to testosterone; this leads to sex, reproduction, and proliferation of our species.

The following is a list of physical and behavioral traits that studies have identified as attractive to women:

Masculine features. Women prefer the physical features that indicate testosterone, including taller stature, heavier jaw and eyebrow ridge, broader shoulders and narrower hips. You don't have to be 6'2" or have a lantern jaw; some women prefer that, but most simply like a man who's taller or broader than she is.

Emotional control. Testosterone makes men less prone to expressing emotion and gives them a more serious facial expression. Women tend to smile more, cry more easily, or express their excitement in obvious ways.

Confidence. Confidence is masculine. Unlike cockiness or arrogance, which are often used to compensate for insecurity, true confidence is means believing in yourself and refusing to allow fear stop you from getting what you want. People who use testosterone supplements report feeling more confident. Confidence puts other people (including women) at ease.

Ambition. Whether you want to run the world or just run your own business, ambition reflects confidence and is very sexy in men. Ambitious men have a plan and follow through with it. Women like that.

Status. Women are attracted to high-status men. This is why CEOs, politicians, movie stars, and musicians have little trouble getting dates. Status indicates confidence, ambition, and talent. On a deeper level, it represents power and resources to protect a woman and her young. Indicators of status include occupations that involve high education, high pay, leadership, or fame.

Wealth. While not as attractive as status, wealth is another indicator of status. It appeals to some women because it represents security. However, wealth isn't as important to women as men think it is. For example, one study found that while some women prefer men with flashy or expensive cars for dating, when it comes to relationships or marriage, women prefer men with regular cars.[2] Why? Flashy cars say "player," not "father."

These traits are attractive to women because they represent masculinity and they represent **power.** Power isn't about snapping your fingers and getting whatever you want – power is knowing you can make things happen in your life anytime you choose. Problem Solvers are masculine and powerful, regardless of how tall or wealthy they are. Complainers come off powerless and whiney – not sexy!

You're a man and you have lots of testosterone. That means you are, ipso facto, attractive to women. If you aren't attracting the women you want, you aren't letting your masculinity shine through. Work on cultivating the above traits. You don't need to have all of them. Instead, capitalize on the ones you have and work on the rest. Some of these traits, like tall stature or wealth, are hard to come by. But the rest of them are well within your control.

In the end, what women really want isn't a CEO, a rich guy, or a guy with a smokin' hot body – they want a masculine man who makes them feel safe and cared for. When men don't realize their full power as men, women fear they'll have to take care of everything, and this stresses them out.

Dating Advice from Men

If you read advice from male dating gurus who teach men how to attract women, some of them will give you the following advice:

- Pretend to have the traits of an "alpha male"
- Be "cocky and funny"
- "Neg" women (i.e. deliver a small insult to show you aren't intimidated by her)
- Create fake stories or other gambits to get a woman to talk to you
- Show up with other attractive women to make a woman jealous (and thus interested)
- Act like you don't care for a woman or need her

When you examine these ploys, you will notice that they are attempts to create the appearance of emotional control, confidence, or other Attraction 101 traits. Some of these ploys are harmless, but others are gamey or disingenuous. Be cautious – you never want to be the guy who has to resort to games or manipulative behavior to get a woman's attention. Games and ploys, whether performed by men or women, are for people who feel powerless with the other sex.

Games and ploys, whether performed by men or women, are for people who feel powerless with the other sex.

Masculinity is attractive on its own. It does not need ploys. And once you attract women, you will need to keep them interested if you want to succeed with them. The next section will show you how.

Attraction 201: What Keeps Women Interested?

Attracting a woman is one thing. Keeping her interest and having an enjoyable time with her – i.e. succeeding with her – is quite another. Whether you're looking for NSA or a wife, attracting women with your strong jaw and great job is just the beginning. There are plenty of good-looking dudes who don't get what they want out of dating, just as there are plenty of high-status men who've have had numerous marriages and numerous ugly, expensive divorces. And there are plenty of average looking, average-status guys who are getting dates, getting laid, and/or enjoying their marriages, all with women they want to be with.

What's so special about these guys? Why do they succeed with women? Because not only do they attract women initially – i.e. they have some Attraction 101 traits – they also have other important traits that make women feel comfortable around them. The following section discusses these other important traits.

They Like Women

Men who succeed with women, like women. They like women for who they are and accept, even enjoy, that they're different from men. Of course, these men are human and may dislike certain women, or may find some feminine behavior baffling, but they generally like women and enjoy their company. Moreover, these men like women in general, not just women they're attracted to, not just hot women, not just their mothers – women, period.

On the other hand, men who don't like women complain that women are difficult, stupid, or untrustworthy. Or they fawn over beautiful women while paying no attention to other women. When confronted, these men will argue vehemently that they "love" women. In most cases these men don't love women, they're attracted to women. In other words, they're heterosexual. Being heterosexual doesn't mean a man likes women.

Being heterosexual doesn't mean a man likes women.

Some men who write dating advice for men – especially internet-based advice – don't trust women. They feel dating is unfair to men or that women only want your money. These advice-givers are the worst kind of Complainers. Don't let their lousy attitudes hinder your success with women. A Problem Solver doesn't bitch about women; he aims to *understand* them. Sure, he gets frustrated; but that frustration motivates him to look for a solution.

Why do men who like and trust women succeed with them? Because they have a Problem Solver's attitude. A Problem Solver knows that no matter what happens with a woman, he will handle it and learn from it. He also knows that just because one or two women caused him grief doesn't mean all of them will.

In general, if you can find value in women as a group, you'll have much greater success with the women who matter most to you. If you find you don't trust women as much as you'd like to, review Chapters 1-2.

They Respect Women

In addition to liking women, men who succeed with women treat women with respect. They're chivalrous and they're tolerant. These men may not always understand women's behavior, but they accept it nonetheless.

For example, most women like clothes and shoes and will spend money on them. This probably makes little sense to you – you don't own a lot of clothes and hate to shop, right? A man who respects women knows women like these things and doesn't criticize them for it. Likewise, a woman shouldn't knock you for enjoying sports or spending money on iPhones, video games, or motorcycles.

A Problem Solver doesn't freak out because a woman has periods, cramps, or "female issues." Sure, he doesn't need to hear every detail, but such things are an unavoidable part of being female, and to treat them as disgusting is to say women are disgusting.

Finally Problem Solvers aren't threatened by women and don't feel resentful of women in positions of power. They admire women who are smart, successful, or really good at tennis. They like women who like sex and don't call them sluts for being sexual or wearing short skirts, nor do they kiss and tell.

Remember: who you are *anywhere* is who you are *everywhere*. A man who respects women in general is a man who will succeed with the women he chooses to be with.

They Have Women Friends

Men who succeed with women often have women friends or involve women in their social group. This doesn't mean they go shopping with women or sit around and talk about shoes. Nor does it mean a man can't enjoy a night with the guys. It means they aren't opposed to having women friends or including women in their social activities, including women they aren't interested in dating.

Remember Harry's speech about how men and women can't be friends in *When Harry Met Sally*? Bullshit. Of course they can. The trick is to choose women you don't have much desire to date or sleep with. Men who figure this out realize they get something from the female friendship that they may not get from their guy friends. Plus, befriending women means more access to their female friends, which means more options for the single guy.

They Have Good Attitudes

As I discussed in Chapter 1, a bad attitude is a major game-killer. Men who succeed with women are generally Problem Solvers, not Complainers, at least in terms of their dating and relationships. Getting your attitude in check is the first and most important step toward success with women.

You can distill the message of this chapter into one simple formula, and that is:

Success with Women = Masculinity + Respecting Women

Read a woman's romance novel sometime. Or, find out who the most popular male movie stars are. Generally, these men have some sort of masculine, Attraction 101 traits along with women-friendly, Attraction 201 traits. Having only one or the other creates problems, and that's what the next chapter is about.

7) THE TESTOSTERONE EFFECT, PART TWO: BAD BOYS, NICE GUYS, AND TOO NICE GUYS

If there's anything that mystifies men, it's why women seem to go for certain guys and not others, even when the "certain guys" don't seem all that great. For example, a woman says she wants a good guy who will treat her well, but when she finds one who does, she dumps him for some asshole who treats her like crap. In the same vein, here are some related quotes I've heard from men:

> *"Women don't appreciate nice guys."*
>
> *"Nice guys finish last."*
>
> *"Women aren't attracted to nice guys; they're attracted to alpha males."*
>
> *"Some women like being treated like crap."*

The above comments are things a Complainer would say, of course. A Problem Solver would never be satisfied with such dismal assumptions about women and dating. He would want to know more.

I spent the last chapter discussing what traits men who succeed with women have. Yet that chapter didn't really explain why Bad Boys, who clearly don't like or respect women, still seem to attract women. Nor did it explain why Nice Guys, who do like and respect women, don't always get the chicks. This chapter will address these issues.

In summarizing what it takes to succeed with women, I offered up this magic formula:

Success with Women = Masculinity + Respecting Women

If a man isn't attracting women, or attracts them but doesn't succeed with them in the bigger sense, it's because he's not following the formula.

Why Do Women Like Bad Boys?

Call them what you want: Jerks, Assholes, Bad Boys, whatever. We've all seen women fall prey to these kinds of men, and wonder why the hell she would bother with a guy like that, especially when she complains about how badly he treats her!

Why do women like Bad Boys? First, it's more accurate to say that women are *attracted* to Bad Boys. And what attracts women to these guys?

Testosterone

As I explained in the last chapter, testosterone makes men masculine. Women are biologically attracted to signs of testosterone because it nearly guarantees the survival of the human race. And while all men have a good dose of testosterone, Bad Boys ooze the stuff from their pores. Some women fall under the spell of this ooze. With testosterone, a little goes a long way – too much makes men very "masculine," but it also makes them poor partners (and not the greatest people, either).

Bad Boys have masculinity, but they do not like women or treat them with respect. They are missing half of the above magic formula. They will attract women, but they won't succeed with them unless they learn to respect them.

When you see a woman dating a Bad Boy – i.e. a guy who is not nice or who doesn't treat women right, you may assume she enjoys being treated like crap. This is never the case. Nobody likes being treated poorly. She is simply attracted to the Bad Boy and will put up with his bad behavior because of her strong attraction.

She puts too much emphasis on physical chemistry, and not enough on compatibility. In other words, she has low standards. And, often, people learn to raise their standards when they tire of being treated poorly.

Men can fall prey to this too. Have you ever dated a gorgeous woman who was nuts or a total bitch? Because the attraction to her feminine traits was so strong, you tolerated her poor treatment, but you didn't like it.

Fortunately, our biological drives to reproduce don't have to control our behavior. Once we become aware of them, we can choose how to handle them. A woman might find the ultra-masculine man hot, but she can choose to ignore such instincts because she knows he's not a good match for her in the long run.

Psychology

Although testosterone is a powerful attractor, another reason some women are drawn to Bad Boys is more psychological in nature. While we choose our partners for conscious reasons (they're attractive, they're nice, they share our values, etc), there is also a subtle unconscious part of us that influences our choices. Often, people will choose partners who remind them of one or both parents, especially if the relationship with the parent was difficult. For example, a woman whose father was abusive may unwittingly choose abusive partners. Or, if a woman's father was unfaithful to her mother, she may choose an unfaithful man. She chooses these Bad Boys as an attempt to come to terms with her issues.

Why Don't Women Appreciate Nice Guys?

One cannot tackle the mystery of why women like Bad Boys without also discussing Nice Guys. However, first we need to define "Nice Guy." There are two kinds of Nice Guys:

1) Nice Guys

2) Too Nice Guys

This section will deal with #1; #2 will be covered in the next section.

My definition of a Nice Guy is a man who likes women, respects women, and treats women right. He has good character and would make a decent husband and father. Nice Guys aren't perfect (no one is), but they're the kind of guys you can trust with your money, your mother, or your girlfriend. These are the kind of men that I, and every other dating expert I know, want women to choose. And a true Nice Guy is also masculine. He succeeds with women.

Women do appreciate Nice Guys. Some women appreciate them from the get-go – they snap them up, marry them, and have kids. Others, unfortunately, have to learn to appreciate Nice Guys the hard way. If you're a Nice Guy who's been with women who didn't appreciate you, here are some reasons why.

She's Still in her Bad Boy Stage

If a woman is still hung up on Bad Boys, no amount of good treatment will help and your good deeds will go unappreciated. As I mentioned above, these women have to learn the hard way that Bad Boys don't make good partners, and that Nice Guys do. And until she figures this out on her own, you're wasting your time with her.

She's Used to Being Treated Poorly

Often, women don't appreciate good treatment because they aren't accustomed to it. Some of these women were raised in homes where love and affection were scarce, or where they were made to feel like they weren't good enough. Then, they get into relationships that reinforce this belief.

This may seem counterintuitive – why don't these women want the opposite of what they grew up with? Unfortunately, it doesn't often work that way. People who were treated like crap growing up often go on to be treated poorly in their adult relationships, or they go on to treat others poorly. That is all they know. This is why a woman may treat you poorly, even when you treat her well. Again, as with women who like Bad Boys, these women struggle in their relationships until they learn, the hard way, to value themselves and to appreciate a man who values them too.

You Thought Your Niceness Could Buy Her Love

Sometimes, I'll hear a man complain that he treated a woman like a queen, just to have her dump him for another guy. Frustrated, he will list all the great things he did for her – things women love – and then come to the conclusion that she simply doesn't appreciate Nice Guys.

Being a true Nice Guy will land you a good woman. But it won't land you every woman. If she dumps you, it's possible that she doesn't appreciate Nice Guys, but it's also very possible that you simply weren't the guy for her. Just because you treat a woman like a queen doesn't guarantee she'll want to be with you.

Treating a woman like a queen doesn't guarantee she'll want to be with you.

Some men believe if they treat a woman great and shower her with the love and gifts she wants, she will stick around. This is true if you're the guy for her, but if you aren't, no amount of great treatment will keep her around. A Problem Solver knows that not all women will want him, no matter how good he is to them. If a woman doesn't appreciate him, he finds one who does.

Contrary to what some people tell you, there's nothing wrong with being a Nice Guy. Nice Guys succeed with women, *as long as they're masculine*. Inadequate masculinity creates other problems, which I address next.

Nice, or Too Nice?

While being a Nice Guy is a great thing, being a Too Nice Guy (TNG) is not. Why is this? Just as Bad Boys exude lots of testosterone, TNGs exude too little. If Bad Boys are missing the "respect women" part of the equation, TNGs are missing the "masculine" part. Without adequate levels of masculinity, a woman may like a man, but she will not be attracted to him.

It's not that TNGs have too little testosterone. They have enough. The problem is that they've buried their masculinity.

The following table illustrates the difference between Nice Guys and TNGs:

Nice Guys	Too Nice Guys (TNGs)
Are comfortable in their masculinity	Try to downplay their masculinity
Turn their backs on bitchy or difficult women	Put up with women who don't treat them right
Stand up for themselves	Let people walk all over them
Prefer equality in relationships, where they share control with women	Let women call the shots because they believe it's the nice thing to do
Accept the ways they're different from women	Apologize for their maleness, as if there's something inherently bad about it
Don't approve of Bad Boys, but don't apologize for them either	Feel they need to make up for the Bad Boys of the world
Do nice things for a woman now and again	Try too hard by showering a woman with gifts, attention, or compliments
Are available when they can be	Are available all the time
Are chivalrous and help women with things like moving heavy objects, fixing broken toilets, or giving financial advice	Allow women to take advantage of their chivalry and wind up giving free handy work to women they get nothing in return from
Say no when a woman's request is something they aren't comfortable with	Say yes to a woman's requests to avoid conflict or angering her
Consider a woman's point of view when making a decision	Let women make the decisions or regularly seek women's advice

When you look at the TNG side of this table, most of these behaviors show a lack of Attraction 101 (masculine) traits, especially confidence. TNGs lack confidence in themselves and their masculinity.

Most men show TNG behaviors now and again. That's fine. However, the more TNG behaviors you engage in, the more you'll struggle with women. You either won't attract them physically, or if you do, they won't respect you enough. Masculinity not only attracts women, it makes them feel calm and safe. TNGs stress women out. When a woman dates a TNG, she feels the burden of having to call the shots, of watching her man not stand up for himself.

Why are TNGs the Way They Are?

Often, the TNG is the way he is because he's formed negative associations with masculinity. This can happen when a man grows up with no Nice Guy role model in his life, perhaps because his father was a Bad Boy who mistreated him or his mother, or abandoned them altogether. Other TNGs were bullied in their youths for not being "male" enough. For these men, masculinity = Jerk. So they downplay their masculinity.

For the record, I happen to like TNGs. Many women do. If forced to choose, I'd take "respects women" over "masculine" any day. It's easier to expand a TNG's masculine side than it is to teach a Bad Boy to respect women. However, I'd prefer to have both halves of the equation, and so do other women.

If you find that you have a TNG streak in you, consider those things that may have influenced you to be Too Nice. Then, make some behavioral adjustments. Cultivate your Attraction 101 masculine traits and follow the lead of Nice Guys. When you do this, you give women what they want. Confidence is very attractive to women and is something any man can get. However, most people don't realize that confidence isn't something you just "have" or "don't have" – it's something you *build*. How? Through trial and error. If something isn't working, keep trying new things until it does work.

Beware the Pendulum

One mistake I see some men make is to "pendulum" – i.e. once their TNG behavior makes them feel walked on, taken advantage of, or not appreciated, they go completely in the other direction and turn into defensive Jerks who don't trust women. This is counterproductive. Remember: you need both halves of the magic formula to succeed with women.

Dating is a Learning Process

One important reason we date is to learn, through trial and error, what kind of person we would be happy with. In this process, we may make poor decisions and pick some pretty inappropriate people instead of the people who would be best for us. Women fall for Bad Boys and men fall for Crazy Hot Girls. It's all part of the learning process. If you meet a woman who likes Bad Boys or who doesn't appreciate Nice Guys, she's learning too. Move on, and keep looking until you find a woman who appreciates you.

8) DIFFICULT WOMEN

You've probably had times when you felt like women were difficult. Who hasn't? However, the majority of the time you can probably acknowledge that, with a few exceptions, most women are reasonable creatures. These reasonable creatures may differ from you, but you get along with them most of the time and work through any conflicts.

This chapter isn't about those women.

Some women are downright difficult. Difficult women are the ones who challenge men, confuse men, and drive men crazy. They're the ones who give women a bad name, who contribute to a man's bad attitude about dating, who make you want to pull your hair out or give up women altogether.

There are many kinds of difficult women, and many different ways a woman can be difficult. This chapter will focus on the difficult women you may come across in dating, and how to deal with them.

The Beauty

While not all beautiful women are difficult, a Beauty can have a strong effect on men. You've probably had a time in your life when a Beauty had you tongue-tied, intimidated you, or had you doing things you never thought you would do. Perhaps you've dated a Beauty and she turned out to be someone who drove you crazy. Or, perhaps you've always longed to date a Beauty, but they've never given you the time of day.

Beauty is tricky. It's great to look at, but getting involved with the wrong Beauty can get you into a heap of trouble. Generally speaking, when a man encounters a beautiful woman, he may do one of two things:

1. **Put her on a pedestal.** He may admire her from afar, failing to imagine how any man wouldn't bend over backwards for her. He compliments her looks (perhaps too many times), looks at her in wonderment, makes comments that he can't believe a girl like her would give a guy like him a chance. He trips over himself to do things for her. If he continues dating her, he may put up with negative behaviors from her, including bitchiness, flakiness, or other crap, because he's so attracted to her.

2. **Try to knock her off her pedestal.** Some men aren't so easily swayed. This man knows that beautiful women have power and are used to getting hit on. He won't be suckered, so he ignores her at first, refusing to fall prey to her charms, or if speaking to her, he treats her like she's nothing special, or even challenges or "negs" her. If dating her, he's on the defense, waiting to see if she'll take advantage of him. Some men won't date Beauties, believing they're all crazy or used to getting whatever they want.

Too Nice Guys, inexperienced guys, and guys who aren't used to getting a lot of attention from women, especially beautiful women, are more likely to go with #1. Not-so-nice guys, guys who've been burned, and players tend to go with #2. However, a Problem Solver knows that both of these approaches are ineffective. Why? Because both give Beauties far too much power. In truth, the only power a Beauty has is the power that YOU give her.

A Beauty only has the power YOU give her.

Yes, a Beauty is used to a lot of attention and admiration from men. And to many men, this seems like an ideal situation – all she has to do is look hot, and she will have droves of men to choose from! Lucky her! Yet, being beautiful has a dark side, in that the vast majority of these men pursue her only because of how she looks and don't give a rat's ass about the real her. And most Beauties figure this out over time.

Imagine, for a moment, that you are famous and fabulously wealthy. You would soon find yourself with a lot of women to choose from, some of whom would be hot or otherwise impressive. Would you feel flattered? Hell, yes! But then, over time, you would realize that most of these women aren't attracted to you – they're attracted to your fame, your money, your status, and what it can do for them. They don't care about you. Not a good feeling, right? This is what beautiful women have to contend with every day.

The way to handle a Beauty is to avoid making the classic mistake of placing too much emphasis on physical chemistry, as I discussed in Chapter 4. You must put aside any powerful effects she may have on you, treat her with respect, and get to know her enough to find out if there's enough compatibility between you to bother. If a Beauty treats you with disrespect, flirts too much with other men, or behaves in a crazy or demanding way, dump her. It's that simple.

Yes, some Beauties are as shallow as a kiddie pool. Why? Because they've been raised to believe that they're not only beautiful, but that their beauty is the only thing that's worthwhile about them. And that's sad.

If you find yourself attracted to or involved with a Beauty, try to see past her looks. Find out what makes her tick. And keep your standards up – if she doesn't click with you, move on.

The Bitch

Every man has run across a bitch at some point. Perhaps she's the woman who bit your head off when you tried to talk to her at a bar. Or, she's the ex-girlfriend who criticized everything you did. It only takes one or two verbal lashings from a Bitch to make you wary of women. I know – I've been stung hard by Bitches too. It isn't fun.

Bitches are mean. They're critical. They're defensive. They yell. They call you names. They talk trash about other people. In a nutshell, they're ANGRY. They're angry at men, or they're angry at the world.

The question is, why?

Because they've been hurt, over and over again. Bitches wear their bitchiness like a shield, hoping to ward off any more hurt and pain than they've already experienced. Sometimes, this hurt and pain stems from being hurt by men. Other times, it stems from childhood, when we are all vulnerable to the unkind actions of friends, family members, or schoolmates. Unfortunately, the Bitch's "shield" may protect her from pain, but it also protects her from ever finding love and happiness.

Bitches are Complainers, not Problem Solvers. They've donned a bad attitude and are still hauling around the 500-pound pack of past baggage. And that's their choice.

Some Bitches come off opinionated or feisty at first, which can be sexy. But watch her to see if Ms. Feisty is really just a Bitch in disguise. Watch how she treats people – if she's rude to them, she'll be rude to you eventually.

A Problem Solver knows a Bitch's behavior isn't about him. He stands up to her without overreacting to her anger. Ultimately, he decides whether a woman's negative side is worth his time or not.

The Emotional Wreck

Emotional Wrecks are women with emotional problems. More accurately, these women aren't aware of their problems or refuse to get help for them. Emotional problems can come in a variety of packages, such as extreme mood swings, addictions, excessive jealousy or possessiveness, or manipulative behaviors.

All women have their ups and downs, but Emotional Wrecks have them much worse and much more often.

The reasons men get involved with these women are psychologically complex, too complex to elaborate on here, but here are a couple of common scenarios:

Blinding chemistry. As I've said, chemistry is powerful stuff. If it hits a man hard, he may ignore the warning signs that a woman has a lot of problems. And, oddly, men have told me the sex can be really amazing with an Emotional Wreck, at least early on. Then, he's hooked in and must navigate the extreme ups and downs of an incompatible relationship.

Some men are Rescuers. Men who are kind-hearted and emotionally tough may attract an Emotional Wreck. She's drawn to his unconditional love; he's drawn to a need to help or fix her. Because the Rescuer has the strength to deal with the ups and downs, he may stick by her side no matter what. But while a Rescuer's heart is in the right place, rescue missions don't work. You know the adage: she has to want to change.

Emotional Wrecks did not get that way on their own. Often, these women were abused as children: physically, emotionally, and/or sexually. While this type of trauma affects every woman differently, it affects them dramatically, especially in their relationships with men. Even when there was no overt abuse, many Emotional Wrecks have experienced difficult or traumatic events in their lives, or may suffer from psychological disorders that haven't been properly treated, including anxiety, depression, addictions, or eating disorders.

Not all women who've been through difficulties are Emotional Wrecks. The key issues are how they choose to deal with their problems and whether or not they get help.

A Problem Solver focuses on women he's compatible with, who have problems he can easily deal with. He also doesn't let negative past experiences with an Emotional Wreck damage him and his future relationships; he learns from it and moves on.

As frustrating as difficult women can be, it's important to understand where they're coming from and realize their behavior isn't your fault or responsibility. However you choose to handle the difficult women you've known, or will meet in the future, avoid taking the Complainer's path and developing resentment toward them. A Problem Solver doesn't take on other people's problems; he does his best to understand and then do what's best for him.

SUCCESS
AND
THE APPROACH

9) METHODS TO MEETING WOMEN

Okay. So you've built a strong foundation by getting into a successful mindset, and you've mastered the psychology of women. Now, it's time to get out there and meet women. But before I launch into the *where* and *how* of meeting women, I want to discuss method. Why is this necessary? Because there are different methods to meeting women, and different men need different methods.

Meeting women is easier for some men, harder for others. Some men thrive on talking to women or perusing an internet dating site for women to chat with. Others dread it, either because approaching women makes them nervous or because they aren't comfortable talking to a bunch of strangers. Why this difference?

Two Kinds of Men

There are two kinds of men: extroverts and introverts. Extroverts are "external" people. They derive their energy from the people and things outside of them, and they're typically talkative and people-oriented. They enjoy meeting new people, they thrive at parties, and they tend to have a wide social circle.

Introverts are "internal" people. They derive their energy from the thoughts and ideas inside of them, and they're typically quiet and idea-oriented. Introverts like people, but they find crowds, parties, and socializing tiring, and tend to have a small social circle of close friends.

Introversion and extroversion are facets of human personality. Neither of these personality styles is better than the other, and both are attractive to women. Some women prefer outgoing, life-of-the-party men; others, like me, prefer quiet, reserved men. However, due to their natures, introverts tend to struggle more than extroverts with meeting women. They require a different method than extroverts do.

A Problem Solver doesn't complain about his personality style or that it doesn't work for meeting women. He embraces who he is and learns to adjust his game accordingly.

Two Methods for Meeting Women

There are many ways to meet women. Some methods work well for some men, but not so well for other men. Generally speaking, when looking to meet women, most dating experts will push one of two methods: the Numbers Method or the Targeted Method.

- **The Numbers Method.** With the Numbers Method, you approach, talk to, meet, or email (if online) as many attractive women as you can. Numbers Method advocates view dating as a numbers game, where the assumption is if you keep trying, eventually one will say yes. Here, you widen your net of possible women and get skilled at approaching women. But the down side is you will face rejection much more often.

- **The Targeted Method.** With the Targeted Method, you approach, talk to, meet, or email (if online) far fewer women, but you do so after carefully assessing whether you believe she's a good bet. In other words, you target women who are closer to your type and/or more likely to say yes. Here, you work with a narrower selection of women, but your odds are greater with each woman.

Generally speaking, the Numbers Method works better for extroverted men, especially if they are bold, highly social, or unusually confident – your salesman types. Being so people-oriented, these men have little problem striking up conversation with women they don't know, and don't often take it too personally if they don't get a date out of it. For them, interacting with women is half the fun. The Numbers Method is often pushed by male dating gurus because it's a way to increase options, sharpen skills, and learn to face rejection.

Alternatively, the Targeted Method generally works better for introverts, especially if they're shy, reserved, or simply uncomfortable approaching that many women. They prefer to save their efforts for a woman they connect with instead of exhausting themselves by trying to talk with tons of women. The Targeted Method also means facing less rejection.

Numbers Method Techniques

If the Numbers Method appeals to you and you have the personality, go for it. Take advantage of your natural extroversion and gift of gab. Talk to women as you stand in line for coffee or as you pick out your favorite cereal at the grocery store. At parties, talk to as many women as feels natural to you. You don't have to hit on them or ask them out; just chat them up and see what happens. If you like them and they seem friendly, ask for an email address or a number. Online, email a bunch of interesting women and see what happens.

However, this method can backfire if you don't abide by a few rules. First, while it's okay to approach women when you're out and about, you don't want to make them uncomfortable. Focus on conversing with a woman and making her feel comfortable, rather than hitting on her or asking her out. If she's responsive to conversation, then make you move. Also, some women will not be receptive to talking to you, for a variety of possible reasons. If she seems busy, uninterested, or even downright hostile, don't take this personally; just leave her alone and move on.

Second, being a Numbers Method guy is great, but beware of being indiscriminate. While it's okay to approach lots of women, a woman doesn't want to feel like she's just one of a million women you hit on that day. And believe me, women can sense these things. Talk to women in a friendly way, but only make your move if you like something about her or if you feel a good connection.

Third, don't hit on a bunch of women who know one another. If you belong to a social group that includes single women, or work with many single women, it's okay to chat with all of them, but only make your move with the one you like most. Why? Because women talk. If you hit on all of them, they'll assume you don't find any of them special, that you're looking for just any woman.

Example

J.J. was a Numbers Method guy. He was cute, successful, and a true extrovert; he was outgoing and could talk to any woman in any situation. After a breakup, J.J. joined a co-ed softball team. He found many of the women on this team attractive and, over time, he hit on each of them. By "hit on," I mean he asked them out or otherwise showed interest in them. These women talked with one another and realized they'd all been hit on by J.J. How many of these women did J.J. score a date with? Zero.

Where did J.J. go wrong? He hit on too many girls in the same social circle. Doing so made him look like he was desperate, like any woman would do. After all, the odds of all those women being good for J.J. were pretty slim. If the women were unacquainted, J.J. could have pulled this off. Instead, he should have gotten to know all the women as friends, then, if he sensed a connection with one of them, made his move.

If you are in the fortunate position of having lots of single women in your social group or workplace, at first they may all look enticing to you. Don't take the bait. Choose carefully; if you fail with one, you may get away with one more, but after that, you become That Guy.

Targeted Method Techniques

When you use the Targeted Method, you will not approach tons of strange women, nor will you ask a woman out until you have a pretty good chance she will say yes. This means targeting women you have good odds with. And knowing which women you have good odds with takes patience and a good eye.

First, the foundation of the Targeted Method is getting to know women before you make a move. You won't date women you run into on the street. Instead, focus on women you meet at work, through friends, or even online – i.e. in situations where you can get to know her over a period of time. This increases the odds of getting a yes from her.

Second, target the women you like most. It's not enough that she's cute or single; look for a connection with her, a sense of mutual attraction, or that you simply like her more than other women. Although liking a woman does not guarantee she'll like you back, it does increase your odds. Women like to know they were chosen over other women.

Finally, target the women you are most likely to succeed with. Avoid women who are far better looking than you, who are seeing other men, who are very different than you, or who show no signs of interest in you. If dating online, don't email women if you don't have the criteria they're looking for. If you have a social circle that includes women, figure out which ones potentially interest you. Get to know them, talk to them. Assess who is most interesting to you, and who seems interested in you.

The Targeted Method takes patience. There may be long periods in which you don't date because you're holding out for a woman you have higher odds with.

Example

Corey and Evangeline met at their book group. Corey was a true introvert – quiet, reserved, hard to get to know. He thought Evangeline was cute from the very start, but he did not reveal his interest yet. Instead, Corey got to know Evangeline over time. At book club meetings, they often sat next to one another, and established a friendship. They became friends on Facebook. After about two months, Corey sensed Evangeline felt as he did and ask her out. She said yes. They eventually got married.

Corey took the Targeted Method. He identified a woman he was interested in, got to know her, established that there was a connection, and then made his move. In this case, Corey took a long time to make his move, even longer than the average Targeted Method guy. But it paid off – not only did he get a date, he found the girl for him.

Corey was also a Problem Solver. With his quiet nature, he wasn't the life of the party and didn't meet tons of women. But he figured out how to adjust his pickup style to work with his personality, and was able to get what he wanted.

Overall, whether you choose the Numbers Method, the Targeted Method, or your own custom method, do what feels right to you. Ultimately, the best method is the one that works.

10) DETECTING INTEREST

No matter what your personality or which method you use to meet women, you will need to learn how to detect when a woman is (or isn't) interested. Next to cultivating a Problem Solver's mindset, learning to read women is one of the most important skills you can learn as a guy. With this skill, you'll be able to better identify women who may be interested in you, which increases your chances of getting dates. You'll be a better conversationalist, making her feel more comfortable with you. And, just as importantly, you'll sense when a woman isn't that interested, greatly reducing rejection and frustration. Not a bad deal, huh?

Having said that, knowing when a woman is interested in you, rather than simply being nice or friendly, is not easy. You guys have it tough: research shows that, on average, men have a harder time reading people than women do. In other words, detecting interest (and lack of it) in the other sex can be a bit harder for men than for women. And, to make things even more challenging, women may give off more confusing signals than men.[3] So if you've ever misjudged a woman's interest, one way or the other, you aren't alone.

Some men have a knack for reading women; these men have little trouble attracting women. Other men seem to have no woman-reading ability whatsoever – they hit on women who clearly aren't interested in them or refuse to make a move when a woman has done everything but take her clothes off. Most men fall somewhere in the middle of these two extremes. A Problem Solver doesn't complain about how hard it is to read women – instead, he learns to read them. Fortunately, the ability to read women is a *skill* – and like all skills, you'll get better at it with practice.

This chapter will cover the signs that a woman is interested. Overall, there are three ways through which you can detect interest in women: body language, eye contact, and conversation.

Body Language

Despite humans having such advanced language skills, 80% of our communication is non-verbal. In this way, we are still animals. Non-verbal communication is faster and more immediate than spoken language. It's also more intuitive, more subtle, and far more honest than spoken language. Body language can tell us most of what we need to know in a situation – the problem is that with our culture's emphasis on the intellect we have stopped paying attention to this more intuitive knowledge.

There have probably been times when you've "sensed" that a woman was interested in you. At those times, you were unconsciously reading her body language without realizing it. Once you learn to recognize the signs on a conscious level, understanding women becomes something you will get better and better at.

Body Language Signs of Interest

Here are body language signs to look for in women:

- **Looking.** If a woman looks at you more than once, or you catch her checking you out, this is a potential sign she's attracted to you.

- **Smiling.** Women smile when they like a guy. The smile will be a "whole face" smile where the eyes crinkle, not just a polite "lips only" smile.

- **Eyebrow flash.** If a woman looks at you and her eyebrows go up, even briefly, that's a sign she finds you attractive.

- **Dilated pupils.** This is a tougher sign to see, but if you notice a woman's pupils enlarge when she talks to you, she likes what she sees.

- **Proximity.** She may walk by you, sit near you, or seem to be nearby often, more often than you'd expect by chance. Likewise, if you frequent a place and then you start seeing a woman show up there more, it may not be a coincidence.

- **Hair toss.** She'll toss or flip her hair, or twirl it around finger.

- **Touching or hitting.** If she touches your arm or pretty much anywhere else, or if she hits you playfully, that's good. Women don't touch men they don't like.

- **Facing you.** If she sits or stands facing you, that's good. She doesn't have to face you completely.

Do these signs guarantee that you're in? Unfortunately, no. She may have a boyfriend, or in some cases she may like you but not be attracted to you. These signs mean that you have a chance. And the more signs you see, the better your chances. Likewise, if you don't see these signs, she probably isn't interested.

At first, you'll find looking for signs of interest a bit overwhelming. But eventually you'll start to get the hang of it as it becomes more intuitive.

Eye Contact

Like body language, eye contact is also a form of non-verbal communication, but it's so powerful that it deserves its own category. The eyes can tell you a *lot*. Eye contact is a powerful way that people telegraph their emotions, including their attraction. Because eye contact is so powerful, people typically avoid it or keep it to a minimum with strangers. Ever been in an elevator? People will go out of their way to avoid eye contact in one because they're trapped in a small space together. Go to your local mall and try to make eye contact with people – most people will meet your eyes briefly, but no longer than that.

The following table provides a cheat-sheet on what eye contact can mean:

Type of Eye Contact	How Long it Lasts	What it Means
Brief	< 1 second	"You exist." "I see you."
Longer	1-2 seconds	"You're kind of attractive." "You're interesting." "I recognize you."
Extended	3+ seconds	"You're very attractive." "I'm definitely interested." "You affect me."

Brief eye contact is for the average person. It's a way to acknowledge that person. Anything longer than a split second is uncomfortable, and therefore meaningful. With women, brief eye contact means she's not interested.

Longer eye contact is a little more interesting. It often signifies potential interest or recognition of an attractive person. We look longer at what we find attractive or interesting – this is true for all people, even infants. Longer eye contact is also used when people recognize one another, as with acquaintances or colleagues, in which case the eye contact is often followed by a nod or hello. Longer eye contact from a woman means she's checking you out, and could be interested.

Extended eye contact is the good stuff. It goes beyond our comfort zone, and can be powerful and highly telling. If a woman makes eye contact with you for this long, pay attention because it usually indicates significant levels of interest or attraction. If she makes extended eye contact with you more than once, it's time to make a move. If she does so and smiles too, then for the love of

God go talk to her! It doesn't matter who initiates extended eye contact, but if she does, that's an even better sign.

Finally, watch how she breaks eye contact, assuming she breaks it before you do (and she probably will) – if she looks down, she may be shy, but if she looks to the side, she's probably not interested. Shy women have a difficult time with eye contact, so look for other subtle signs of interest.

Conversation

Even though 80% of what we communicate is non-verbal, you can still tell a lot about a woman's interest by what she says when you talk to her. Here are some conversational signs that she's interested:

Conversational Signs of Interest

- **She initiates conversation.** Her talking to you is good, but her starting a conversation with you is even better.

- **She asks you about yourself.** It's not enough for a woman to listen when you talk, which she'll do out of politeness, especially if you're a talker. But if she continues the conversation and asks questions, that's a good sign.

- **She compliments you.** This is always a good sign.

- **She remembers you.** A potentially interested woman will often remember your name or reference something you said in a previous conversation. Another good sign is when she recognizes you from a class, restaurant, the gym, or pretty much anywhere. It means she noticed you.

- **She seems nervous.** Another very good sign. Look for fidgeting, stuttering, giggling, or nervous chatter.

- **She laughs.** She laughs at your humor or seems to enjoy your company.

Again, none of these signs guarantees she's interested. They're just good signs, and noticing them helps you increase your odds of success. As with all signs of interest, look for a pattern of signs rather than focusing on any one sign.

Detecting a Lack of Interest

While it's important to know the signs that a woman is interested, it's also important to recognize the signs that a woman is NOT interested. These signs will vary depending on what stage you are in the dating process.

Before You Talk to Her

- **Brief or no eye contact.** If you make eye contact with a woman, watch what she does. If she looks away quickly and doesn't look at you again, she isn't interested. However, if she makes longer eye contact with you and looks away, or looks away quickly but then makes eye contact with you again, she may be shy. If you want to test the waters, smile at her and see if she responds.

- **No smile.** A serious expression isn't always a bad sign, but it isn't a good sign either. She may be in a bad mood, or just deep in thought. Again, you can test the waters by smiling at her. If she gives you a nice smile, that's a decent sign. If she doesn't smile, gives you a very brief smile, or gives you a fake smile, leave her be.

- **Closed body language.** If a woman's body language appears closed off, she isn't interested, at least not yet. Closed body language includes a serious face, crossed arms, or her body is turned away from you (even if her head is facing you).

After Talking to Her

- **She doesn't seem interested in the conversation.** If a woman gives brief or dull answers, looks down, looks around, avoids eye contact, or her body is turned away (as if she's looking to walk away), wrap up the conversation and let her go.

- **She talks about other guys.** If she mentions other men to you, whether men she's seeing or men she's possibly interested in, even if her commentary is negative, she's not interested. When women like a man, they instinctively avoid bringing up other men.

- **She doesn't return your call or email.** If you get a woman's info and call or email her, she should respond quickly (within a day or two). If she doesn't, she may not be interested, or she's unsure. In this situation, it's okay to try once more if you want to. This may work because she'll see that you're serious. If you don't get a response after the second try, move on.

After You've Gone Out With Her

- **She takes too long to return your calls.** While slow response (more than a couple days) is a mixed bag before you go out with a woman, it's a bad sign after you've gone out.

- **She doesn't want to see you regularly.** If you've been out several times and she doesn't want to see you more regularly (i.e. at least once a week, if not more), she may be somewhat interested, but not interested enough.

- **She's always busy.** A woman who's too busy to see you or spend time with you isn't that interested, regardless of what she tells you. Nowadays, "busy" is a common excuse people use to get out of doing things they don't want to do.

- **She doesn't want to sleep with you.** If you've been dating a while and nothing is happening physically, or she isn't responding to your advances, she's probably not interested in you. This is NOT the same as her wanting to wait to have sex; in that case, she *wants* to have sex and will show you in her way that she wants to, but that she's chosen to wait. Look for *interest* in sex, rather than whether you're having it yet or not.

In most situations, if you see the above signs of disinterest, move on. If you aren't sure, ask. However, with an interested woman, you won't usually have to ask.

What about Mixed Messages?

When a woman never returns your calls or otherwise shows clear signs of disinterest, it's not fun, but at least's it's *clear*. You know where you stand. But sometimes a woman will send "mixed messages" – i.e. signs of interest and disinterest, which can be very confusing.

For example, a woman doesn't return your calls, but then seems really glad to hear from you when you do get a hold of her. Or, she postpones dates because she's too busy to see you, but then acts like you're the center of her world when you do finally see her. To deal with this, abide by the Mixed Messages Rule: when a woman gives you mixed messages, the negative messages are the bottom line. In other words, the lack of returned calls and being to "busy" tell you more than the positive signs.

When a woman gives you mixed messages, the negative ones are the bottom line.

Usually, when a woman gives mixed messages, she has mixed feelings. Words don't always tell the truth, but behavior never lies. Although it's fine to back off and see if she comes around, ultimately you want a woman who knows she's interested in you.

You will find that you can only learn so much about reading women from a book. The best way to learn is to get out there and learn through experience. Intuition and "sensing" things isn't just for women – men too can cultivate this side of themselves and become good people-readers. And when you do, the payoff will be huge.

11) WHERE TO MEET WOMEN

One of the most common questions I get from men is: "Where do I meet women?" Often, men who ask this question are hoping to discover places where attractive single women hang out, as if there are secret locales where these women gather, waiting for men to show up. Many of you have already figured out that, for the most part, there is no such place.

The truth is, you can meet women almost anywhere. What you really seek isn't just places that attract single women, but places that are *conducive* to *actually meeting them*. Psychologically, some places put people at ease, making it easy for you to meet women, while other places don't encourage socializing, making things tougher for you. In this chapter, I provide a list of common venues to meet women, including the pros and cons of each. The next chapter will discuss how to actually make your approach at these places.

For many men, the first place that comes to mind when they think about meeting women is a bar. Why? Bars attract singles, and bars have plenty of alcohol to help these single people get together. But over the years, the many drawbacks of meeting in bars have become obvious. Often, in their online profiles, men will remark that they're "tired of the bar scene." If you feel this way, I'm glad to hear it. Going to bars to meet women is for amateurs. You're beyond that now.

Bars are places to relax after work, watch the game, or drink with your friends. They are NOT places to meet women. Unfortunately, a lot of dating advice written for men revolves around teaching them to meet women at… you guessed it, bars and clubs.

Bars are places to drink with your friends. They are NOT a place to meet women.

Of course, if you're looking for a one-nighter (i.e. NSA), a bar is a potential place to meet a woman who is open to that. But if you're looking for anything else at all, don't bother looking in bars.

Most importantly, if a Problem Solver doesn't know where to meet women or hasn't had good luck, he doesn't give up or keep doing the same thing. Instead, he discovers where other men go to meet women and gives those places a try.

Where Couples Meet: The Latest Statistics

A major online dating site hired a research firm to poll thousands of couples who got married during 2005-2010 and ask them how they met. As you can see from the chart below, most couples (38%) met through work or school, followed by 27% who met through friends or family. Combined, that's two-thirds of couples.

However, when you examine the chart, there is a decent-sized third way that couples meet – through online dating sites. Online dating sites used to comprise only a thin wedge of that pie; today, the number of couples who meet online rises every year and has crept up to 17%, or 1 in 6.

Overall, this chart shows us several things:

1. Work/school and friends are still great ways to meet women

2. Online dating is becoming an increasingly common way to meet women

3. Bars and clubs are a waste of time for meeting women

4. While some suggest that church is good way to meet someone if you're looking for a relationship or marriage, the numbers don't support this. I recommend church or church-related events only if your faith is a major part of your life; otherwise, look elsewhere.

How Recently Married Couples Met

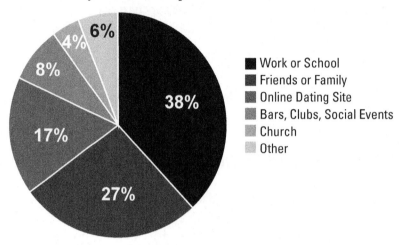

Venues to Meet Women

When you're looking to meet women, you will want to choose places that have the following two criteria:

1) Single women go there
2) The venue encourages socializing and getting to know one another

Below, I present a list of places to meet women, all of which satisfy these two criteria to varying degrees.

Online Dating Sites

More and more couples are meeting online, and the industry has responded by creating numerous dating sites to choose from.

Pros: Lots of single women. And, you know for a fact that the women are interested in dating, and thus it's expected that you contact women for dating purposes. That is not the case with the other places on this list. So while you will face rejection online, it won't be because she's married, has a boyfriend, or isn't there to meet men.

Cons: Online dating can be frustrating and result in disappointment if it isn't done in an optimal way. It requires different expectations and different tactics, all of which I discuss in Chapters 19-24.

Dating sites come in all shapes and sizes, but there are basically three varieties: standard sites, match-based sites, and niche sites.

Standard sites. Standard sites allow you to sign up, create a profile, and begin browsing for, emailing, or instant messaging women. The larger sites have millions of subscribers across the country. One pro is they give you a lot of flexibility. You can browse for free if you aren't sure you're ready to contact women yet, you can choose the criteria you want for your dates, and you can do a variety of searches for women based on those criteria. For example, you can search for blonde women over 5'10" with a master's degree. Another pro is the sheer number of people on these sites, increasing your pool of options. The con of these sites is that you only have a picture and basic profile to go on, which means you will meet a lot of women who aren't your type.

Some of these sites are free, others have reasonable subscription fees. You can try the free sites, but I've found that pay sites tend to attract people who are serious about dating. Examples of standard sites include Match, OkCupid, and PlentyOfFish.

Match-based sites. Match-based sites attempt to pair you with women you're more likely to be compatible with based on your personality, values, and lifestyle. These criteria are assessed through a questionnaire you fill out when you sign up with the service. Then, the site delivers you profiles of women who are good matches for you based on your test profile. The pro is that the matches they send are more likely to be compatible with you, and sites that use this method tend to attract people looking for relationships and marriage. The con is that you don't get to browse freely on the site and the women they send you won't always be your physical type. Examples include eHarmony and Chemistry.

Niche sites. There are many dating sites oriented toward people who share a unique interest or attribute. The idea behind niche sights is to meet people who share qualities that are important to you, such as ethnicity, religion, or a beloved hobby. Below, I list a few examples of niche sites, and what they specialize in:

Niche Dating Site Examples

Ethnicity

- AsianSinglesConnection
- BlackSingles
- IndianMatrimonialNetwork

Religion

- JDate. For Jewish singles.
- CatholicMingle
- ChristianMingle

Single Parents

- SingleParentsMingle

Pets

- DateMyPet
- Purrsonals.com. Social network for cat lovers.

Other Niche Sites

- The Right Stuff. For graduates/faculty of a select group of excellent universities.
- FitnessSingles. For fitness-minded people.
- GreenFriends. For vegetarians and the green-minded.
- Darwin Dating. A site for "beautiful people only."
- STDmatch. For those living with STDs.
- Trek Passions. For those who love Star Trek, Star Wars, or other sci-fi.

This is only a partial list. As you can see, there's something out there for everyone! My general advice is that you should sign up with at least one online dating site to maximize your options. If online dating is the primary way you meet women, then you should aim for two sites: one large site (regular or match-based) and one niche site.

The Workplace

While some consider dating in the workplace a bad idea, you can see from the charts above that it's the most common place singles meet.

Pros: The workplace allows people to get to know one another in an environment they're comfortable in. There's no rush to get a phone number. You can take your time and really get to know a woman over weeks, months, even years. It's easier to meet, and you can find out more about her from coworkers. And if you work at the same place, you may have a lot in common. In other words, at work you can establish if you have compatibility with a woman, rather than just chemistry.

Cons: Some companies have rules about employee relationships, so it's important to know what they are. Also, if things don't work out, you may have to see that person nearly every day, which is uncomfortable. In general, you're better off not dating any woman you deal with on a day-to-day basis. Stick with women who work on other floors, in other departments, or at other sites.

School

Meeting at school isn't just for high school or college kids anymore. These days, a lot of adults take classes in the evenings to bolster their careers, to change fields, or just to learn something new.

Pros: School is another environment that puts people at ease. And, if you're in the same class with a woman, you already have something in common. You also have a reason to talk with her without seeming like you're hitting on her, not to mention something to talk about. Also, you have an entire semester to get to know her before you make your move.

Cons: There isn't a lot of time to chat during class, forcing you to make the most of the time just before or just after class. And if things don't work out, you will have to face her for the remainder of the semester.

Parties and Barbeques

Parties are one way you can meet women through friends. As the stats show, meeting through friends is a very popular way couples meet. Go to every dinner party, birthday party, coed wedding shower, wedding, and pretty much every gig you're invited to. You never know when you'll meet an interesting woman.

Pros: Parties are social environments. Here, it is almost expected that you walk up to a woman you've never met and say hello. This is not true in many other places. You already have two things in common – the reason for attending the party and the mutual friend who invited you – which gives you a conversation opener. Plus, most people are relaxed and enjoying themselves at parties, and having a drink or two never hurts either.

Cons: Parties are tougher for shy or introverted men, and aren't quite as easy as work or school. Also, not every party will have single women or women who interest you. And be cautious about how much you drink – drunkenness always backfires with women. If you need that much alcohol to talk to women, your confidence needs some work.

Social Clubs and Meet-ups

Whatever your interests and hobbies, there are others who share them. They have clubs and meet-ups (e.g. Meetup.com) for cyclists, wine lovers, book lovers, entrepreneurs, and nearly everything else.

Pros: Membership in a club means you already have something in common with a woman, and gives you something to talk about.

Cons: If your interests happen to appeal to men (e.g. team sports or gun collecting) or to married women (e.g. good parenting), this may not be the best method for you to meet women.

Coffee Houses

Coffee and tea joints are the new bars, but without the drunk people and loud music. Lots of people visit them to get their caffeine jolt, to work on their laptops, or to just hang out on a rainy day. They're also a potential place to meet women.

Pros: Coffee joints attract single people, especially those who work from home, because they get lonely being by themselves so much. It's a way to get out of the house, maybe even meet some new people.

Cons: Coffee houses don't encourage socializing as much as the above venues do, and some women only want to read their book or do their work. Thus, you have to be a bit more strategic in how you approach women here.

The Gym

I've had long discussions with men about how to meet someone at the gym. Although the gym isn't a common place for couples to meet, it's tempting for the fitness-oriented, and some couples do meet this way.

Pros: Like attracts like, and two fitness buffs do well together. The gym is a place where a fit man can show his stuff, and where any man can show that he cares about his body. This is attractive to women. Also, the gym is a place where you can see a woman on a regular basis, which makes it a little easier to eventually meet.

Cons: The purpose of a gym is fitness, not socializing. It is inappropriate to simply go up to a woman and talk, and hitting on a woman at a gym is a big no-no. This makes the gym one of the most difficult venues to meet women. Also, if you spend a lot of time in the weight room, there are few women to choose from; most women are in the cardio room (where conversation is difficult) or in classes (where most men fear to tread). As a result, meeting women at the gym requires more skill.

Places of Business

This category includes grocery stores, Target, the bank, or other places most people go to run their errands or take care of other necessities.

Pros: As they say, you never know when or where you'll meet someone interesting, so it pays to be prepared and keep your eyes open for signals. And places of business are a good place to practice conversing with women you don't know. You'll probably never see her again, so what do you have to lose?

Cons: Places of business are the toughest way to meet women. When running errands, most people (men included) aren't prepared to meet the other sex. And if a chance encounter does occur, you only have a short window of time to establish rapport and ask her out. Often, this is just not long enough. However, they're great places to hone your skills and to have some fun with random women.

The following chart summarizes the places to meet women, rating them based on whether they attract single women and whether they're conducive to meeting them. Five represents lots of single women and the most conducive environment, 0 represents few single women and the least conducive environment.

Places to Meet Women, Ranked from 0-5

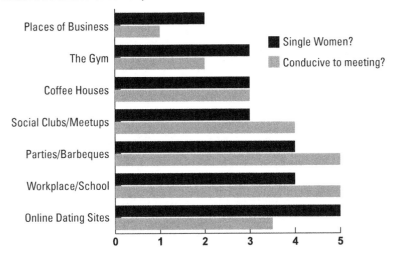

As you can see, some places have more single women than others, and some places make it easier to actually meet them. A Problem Solver takes advantage of those places that make things easier for him; however, he does not let the cons of the more challenging venues stop him. He knows the tougher venues require extra skill and sees that not only as a challenge, but an opportunity to sharpen his skill set.

If you want to meet women, you need to get out of the house, keep your eyes open, and look for opportunities. The next chapter will show you how.

12) HOW TO APPROACH WOMEN

One of the most difficult tasks a man faces in dating is approaching women. If this task seems intimidating or makes you a bit nervous, that's normal. It should make you nervous. Approaching a stranger is uncomfortable enough – but approaching an attractive member of the opposite sex? There are few things in life that are more difficult.

In my second book, *It's Not Him, It's YOU*, I strongly encourage women to initiate contact with men, whether it's through body language or even by starting a conversation. This gives men the green light to make an approach. However, there are still many women who haven't read my book, and just as many women who've been told that it's the man's job to make the first move. What this means is that, often, you will have to make the approach. This chapter will show you how to do so successfully.

The Approach Depends on the Venue

When it comes to approaching women, there is no one way that works all the time. You have to adjust your approach technique depending on the venue. The general rule is this: the less conducive the venue, and the less familiar you are to her, the more you'll need to move slowly and establish rapport. Approaching a woman at a party thrown by a mutual friend is much easier than approaching a woman you've never met at Target.

The less conducive the venue, and the less familiar you are to her, the more you'll need to move slowly and establish rapport.

Why this rule? It all goes back to psychology. To some extent, all humans are naturally wary of strangers; until the stranger shows a basic level of trustworthiness, people will remain wary. Moreover, women are wary of strange men. We have no way of knowing if you're a good guy looking to chat, a weird guy looking to interrupt our alone time, a player looking for his next lay, or a bad man who preys upon women.

Also, humans are highly influenced by their environments. A friend's home filled with people who know him puts us at greater ease than a grocery store filled with random people. Women feel at greater ease in work clothes and makeup than they do in sweaty gym clothes and no makeup. If a woman is at ease, she's easier to meet.

So it's important that you adjust your technique to fit the situation. If the venue is conducive, great. If not, you can still create the necessary conditions for success.

Approach Techniques

You want to approach a woman in a way that's appropriate to the venue, which will make her feel more comfortable and increase your odds of success. Below, I've listed those places I discussed in the last chapter. For each place, I outline some suggestions for how to approach women.

Online Dating Sites

Online dating is an ideal setting for approaching women because the sole purpose of these sites is just that – to meet other singles. However, you and the women who interest you are strangers who haven't established rapport yet. So, unless a woman contacts you first, all online approaches mean approaching a woman before you know if she's interested.

You can email women who interest you, send a "wink" or "hello" to signal interest, or, if the site allows it, instant message women. Email is usually the best choice. Consult Chapter 22 for advice on contacting women online.

The Workplace/School

At the office, dating isn't necessarily your top priority (or hers), but it's still one of the top places that couples meet. At work, you have an excuse to talk to a woman. If she's new, introduce yourself and welcome her aboard. If she's worked there a while but you just met her, say, "Don't you work in marketing? My buddy works there too," or, "How long have you been with the company?" You also have something in common, such as how full the fridge is with people's rotting food or how confusing the new copier is. Make a joke about it. If you have a group happy hour with your coworkers, invite her to join. Whatever way you choose, you will have broken the ice with her.

Go to office happy hours (or start one), attend annual Christmas parties, and join other office social events. Get to know your coworkers and go to lunch with them. Invite the cute girl from accounting to join you all.

Dating at work doesn't have to be just coworkers. You can meet women at work-related conferences, through meetings with external consultants or vendors who deal with your company, or even customers are a possibility. It's probably not a good idea to hit on female customers, but you can talk to them and get to know them. They may come back to your workplace to see you!

Often, with work-related romance, the two people got to know and like each other over time, to the point where it became worth the risk to date at work. However, never hit on or ask out a woman at work until you've gotten to know her and established that she's probably interested. If you do, you risk making things awkward. The less you see her at work, the less this rule applies.

At school, try to talk to your classmates before and after class. Sit next to a woman you find attractive. Ask how she did on the last test. Organize a study group with her and others. Again, as with work, don't rush to go out with her. Get to know her, establish that there's potential mutual interest, then make your move.

Parties and Barbeques

Parties are great settings to approach women because you know some of the same people, and meeting new people is expected. Again, look for signals. Is that cute blonde smiling at you? If so, great. If not, it's still okay to approach strangers at a party.

Say hello, ask her how she's doing, and then ask her how she knows the host (or the bride, groom, or organizer). If you stand near the food or drinks, you can make comments on what she chooses to eat or drink (jokes are okay, but no rude comments!). Say, "Drinking beer at a wine party... I like it!" or, "That guacamole is seriously good. I ate half the bowl already." If you have friends in common at the party, say, "Aren't you Ashley's friend?" or, "Did we meet at Steve's barbeque last year?" Even if you're wrong, the conversation has begun.

You can talk to as few or as many women as you choose at a party. Once you've established rapport with one and sense potential mutual interest, ask for her info.

Social Clubs and Meet-ups

Social clubs and meet-ups are good places to meet women you have something in common with. This common interest provides you a good excuse to initiate conversation and develop a friendship. However, this is an easy setting for conversation, but it's a harder one for dating, as women don't necessarily join clubs and meet-ups looking to date.

If you join a running club, for example, introduce yourself to new women who join the group. If you're new, introduce yourself to as many people as possible. Ask her how long she's been running, if she races, and if so, what distance. If you join a book club meet-up, ask her what she thought about the latest book, or what some of her all-time favorite books are.

The trick is to build rapport with these women and see if something develops. Don't hit on or ask a woman out before you build rapport. If you do, you will become That Guy who hits on every woman. Likewise, don't join a group just to meet women; join out of genuine interest. You'll be much more at ease this way.

To avoid becoming That Guy, build rapport with a woman before asking her out.

Coffee Houses

Coffee joints are a bit more challenging because you don't have an automatic excuse to talk with a woman like you do at any of the above venues. And, most women don't go to a coffee joint to socialize or meet men; they go for their caffeine fix or to work. Here, you will need to look for signs of interest as much as possible. If you don't see them, you can still approach, as long as you keep it brief.

To do this effectively, you will want to perform a Receptivity Test. The Receptivity Test is a quick question or comment you make, followed by a read of her reaction. You will toss out a quick "How are you?" or a brief comment, question, or compliment to a woman. Then, observe her body language. If she smiles, laughs, or otherwise seems reasonably friendly, she's potentially receptive and you can take the next step. If she frowns or seems preoccupied, bored, or annoyed, she isn't receptive – leave her be.

Once you take the next step, continue to gauge her receptivity. And even if she's friendly, don't overstay your welcome. One step at a time.

When you attempt a Receptivity Test, another trick is to look at her, but make sure your body (everything from the shoulders down) is turned away from her. This sends the message that you're just quickly stopping by, which will yield better results. Facing her means you expect more from her, which will make her uncomfortable. If the conversation develops, you will instinctively turn your body toward her.

Another option is to strike up a conversation while waiting in line, waiting for your beverage to be made, or while you add your cream and sugar. You can ask her opinion on which scones are good, if she knows what the heck a macchiato is, or comment that skim milk is no substitute for half-and-half. This is easier because it comes off like you're just being friendly or passing the time, rather than targeting her. I once met a man in line (I was reading The *Onion* and he commented on it); we had a good conversation and then he invited me to join him once we ordered our stuff. I did; we had a great time. Well-played on his part.

If you build good rapport in your first conversation, great. If not, revisit the place and hopefully you'll see her again. The more you frequent a coffee joint, the more you'll recognize regulars, and the more they'll recognize you. You have better odds when a woman recognizes you. I've met a lot of men in coffee houses, but rarely did we talk the first time we saw one another there. Often, it took weeks or even months.

> *Example*
>
> Standing in line for coffee, you notice that the woman in front of you is cute, so you decide to talk to her.
>
> **You:** "Would you mind if I cut in front of you? My caffeine withdrawals are kicking in." (Smile so she knows you're kidding).
>
> **Her:** (Laughs). "Yes, you can cut in."
>
> **You:** "Thanks, I appreciate it." (Don't actually get in front of her, even if she urges you to.)

Leave it at that. If she keeps talking, great. If not, that's okay too. Having talked to her gives you the go-ahead to make another comment to her later on (perhaps that you're feeling much better now that you got your fix), or to speak to her if you see her there another day.

The Gym

Approaching women at the gym is tough. Most people aren't at ease at the gym – they're focused on their workout, they're dressed down, and some may not even want to be there. Many women feel uncomfortable at gyms (especially weight rooms), and don't necessarily feel sexy.

Pretty daunting odds.

Having said that, don't give up hope if you like a girl at your gym. I know couples who've met at the gym. I've heard many men complain about how hard it is to meet women at the gym, but a Problem Solver doesn't complain – he recognizes the challenges and adjusts his technique. The trick is to be very patient, look for signals, and master the Receptivity Test.

First, keep your eye out for women who look at you, make eye contact, or smile. They may not necessarily be interested in a date, but chances are they'll be reasonably friendly if you talk to them. That's a great starting point for a Receptivity Test. If you see the woman you like on a regular basis, that's good – the more she sees you, the more familiar you become to her.

If she hasn't noticed you yet, start with eye contact. This is essentially a non-verbal Receptivity Test – how does she respond after a few tries? If she consistently looks away from you quickly, she isn't interested. If she meets your eyes or seems friendly, good.

Next time, take the Receptivity Test to the next level: smile at her. Does she smile back? If so, work up to a nod or a hello. If she responds and begins to acknowledge you, graduate to a "How are you?" Acknowledge her response, then move along. This is how you avoid coming on too strong. Again, gauge her response. If she responds in an unfriendly way, let her go. If she's friendlier, acknowledge her when you see her next time.

Eventually, one or the both of you, assuming the signs are still there, will start a conversation. This is yet another Receptivity Test. You can keep it simple, like, "How long have you been coming here?" or, "How was your weekend?" or, "It's crowded tonight."

This process may seem painfully slow and arduous to you. But it's like anything – with practice it will become automatic. And remember: the tougher the challenge, the greater the reward.

Moreover, this process works. Sometimes it proceeds quickly, sometimes slowly. Hell, if you manage to converse with a woman you like at the gym, assuming she was at all friendly, you've achieved more than most men ever will. That's already a huge success. If it feels right, asking her out is a natural next step.

What if she's wearing headphones? Headphones mean she isn't up for talking, so don't approach her. You can, however, still make eye contact or smile. Trust me, if she wants to talk, she'll take her ear buds out. When I saw a man I wanted to talk to at the gym, I took one ear bud out when I'd see him to show him I wanted to hear what he had to say.

Example

At the gym, you notice that a woman is wearing a Boston Marathon shirt, and you're a runner. You could say:

You: Hi, I noticed your shirt. You ran the Boston Marathon? [Receptivity Test]

Her: Yeah, two years ago.

You: (Watch her – does she look uninterested or like she needs to leave, or is she facing you, like she's interested in talking briefly?). If the former, say, "Nice, I heard that's a good course," and move along. If the latter, let the conversation take its course.

Always watch her body language. If you sense she doesn't want to talk anymore, let her off the hook and say, "Good talking to you" or, "Cool, well, take it easy." And, again, even if it's going really well, don't overstay your welcome.

Places of Business

With a non-social setting, time constraints, and a complete lack of acquaintance between you and any woman you meet, places of business such as the bank or grocery store are the toughest way to meet women. However, they are a great place to practice your approach and your conversational skills. If you can successfully converse with a woman in this environment, you can do so *anywhere*. And you could wind up getting a date out of it!

When approaching women at places of business, you must make yourself seem as friendly and non-threatening as possible. Remember, she doesn't know what you're about yet. Use your surrounds to generate fun conversation. If waiting in line, comment on how long the line is or on something in her basket. If in the cereal aisle, ask her if she can help you find the Lucky Charms. These are all Receptivity Tests. Keep it to one line and see what she does.

If she ignores you or barely responds, she isn't up for talking, so leave her alone. If she laughs or responds beyond pointing out the box of Lucky Charms, continue the conversation. If she's not interested, she'll resume her shopping. If she is interested, she'll keep trying to talk to you, stay in your area, or walk away but look back at you and smile. In this case, she's probably waiting for you to make a move.

Once you break the ice and feel that the conversation has gone well, you could say, "Hey, I know we haven't known each other all that long, but would you be up for getting a coffee sometime?" This acknowledges the awkwardness of trying to get a stranger to go out with you, and your recognition of that fact will increase her comfort level. You could also offer to give her your number or email, so she doesn't have to risk giving her info to a stranger.

Whatever you do, don't overstay your welcome. Read her. Avoid peppering a woman with comments or questions, which she'll only answer to be polite. Give her an easy out.

Overall, approaching women in places of business is great practice. See what works and what doesn't. If you can chat up a stranger in the electronics department at Wal-Mart, you can probably do anything.

"What if I Get Signals and Then Get Shut Down?"

Yes, this will happen. No matter where you meet or how interested a woman may seem, she may have a boyfriend or may not feel sure about you yet. Don't sweat it. If she hems and haws or says she can't, just smile and say, "Okay" or, "Hey, it was worth a shot." Then, move on. This shows confidence and makes it look like you aren't crushed about it (even if you are). In some cases, she may change her mind down the road.

Also, examine the situation. Did she truly seem interested, or was she just being polite? Learn to tell the difference. In the end, however, dating always involves risk. If you want to reduce rejection, learn to read women and establish rapport before making a move.

Dealing with Unfriendly Women

Occasionally, you may come across a woman who is unfriendly when you approach her. A Problem Solver knows that this will happen and doesn't let it get him down. That's why you perform the Receptivity Test – if she's unfriendly, she isn't receptive. Case closed.

To some extent, if you're a stranger to her, an unfriendly response makes sense. Remember: she doesn't know you or what your intentions are yet. Once she sees you're only making (brief) conversation, she'll relax and probably be polite.

Rudeness is tougher to take. If she's rude, she's having a bad day, isn't a happy person, or has been harassed by men in the past and is overreacting. To avoid this, don't approach women who appear unfriendly, who are in the middle of talking with someone, or who appear busy, preoccupied, or unhappy. Move on to friendlier territory.

In some cases, a woman is unfriendly because a man makes her feel uncomfortable or invades her space. For example, if a woman is sitting at a table in a coffee shop and you start talking with her or, worse, sit down with her, she will not respond well. Why? Because you have essentially forced her into a conversation she may not want to have, and nobody likes that. Instead, utilize the Receptivity Test. If she doesn't seem receptive, move on.

Approaching women is a challenge. But with some good people-reading skills and the ability to adjust your technique depending on the situation, you will greatly increase your odds of success. The more challenging the venue, the more challenging the approach.

The upside of the challenging venues – besides the feeling of triumph you'll get when you get a woman's number – is that once you learn to approach women at these tougher places, you can pretty much approach women anywhere. And once you can do that, your options become practically endless.

SUCCESS
AND DATING

13) ASKING HER OUT

Once you've broken the ice with a woman, detected potential signs of interest from her, and established rapport, it's time to ask her out. The psychology behind two people setting up a first date is complex. You risk putting yourself out there and getting rejected. She risks hurting your feelings, or that you won't turn out to be a good guy. More importantly, even though it's just a date and not a marriage proposal, there's a lot riding on a first date because we all know, deep down, that all great relationships (and all crappy relationships) officially begin with the first date. Once you schedule a date, it's game on.

However, none of these factors should deter you. Why? Because dating always involves some risk. A Problem Solver doesn't let that stop him; he remains aware of the challenges and works around them.

Getting in Contact with Her

These days, you have a lot of options for getting in contact with a woman. The more obvious ways include asking for her number or getting her email address. Email can be a way to test the waters with a woman before asking her out, and can be less awkward for both parties. Most of the men I've dated in the last 10 years have emailed me to ask me out.

What about texting? Keep texting to a minimum. It's a good way to transmit important information quickly, such as when you're running 10 minutes late. It's also a good way to keep in touch with a woman when a phone call isn't a good idea, such as when you're in the middle of a dull meeting. Otherwise, call. Never ask her out or make plans over text – it comes off lazy and impersonal. If you don't want to talk to her, you don't want to date her; put your thumbs to rest and find a girl you feel like calling.

Once you get her info, you can do one of two things: ask her out then and there, or find some way to get in contact with her and ask her out later. The first way is more direct, which is fine if you're feeling bold or sense solid interest on her part. The second way, getting in contact with her first, is less direct, but can be less nerve-wracking for both of you and can be more effective if a woman isn't sure she's interested yet. Do what feels right.

What about Facebook and other social media? It's fine to "friend" a woman on Facebook, especially if you have friends in common and could see yourself being friends with her even if you never date. However, this is better to do with women you're only potentially interested in; once she says yes to a date, avoid friending her until you know how things go.

When to Contact Her

If you get a woman's contact info, when you contact her is your choice. However, remember that the lag time between when you get her info and when you actually contact her says everything about your interest level. If the lag time is:

1-3 days: This is the golden zone. This shows real interest on your part. The sooner you contact her, the more interested you'll seem, and that's okay if she likes you. If you really hit it off, it's okay to contact her within a day. If you're unsure about her interest or fear appearing eager, it's fine to wait a day or two.

4-6 days: This is the gray zone. You're pushing it a little, increasing the risk that she'll think you aren't serious or that she'll lose interest. I advise women that 4-6 days is a bit long to wait, but to give it a chance IF she has a good feeling about you.

7+ days: You waited too long. Let's face it: she's probably given up on you and you probably aren't that interested anyway. That's okay. Toss her card and let it go. If you think you still want to contact her, you can, but prepare yourself for any variety of responses – for example, she may not remember you, or she may get snippy with you.

There are male dating gurus who will tell you to wait more than three days, even as long as a week, to call a woman who gave you her number. I don't advise this. However, sometimes stuff comes up, and it isn't a crime if you don't contact her right away. Just know that the longer you wait, the more likely you are to get a negative response, or no response at all.

What if She Doesn't Respond?

Sometimes a woman will give you her info and then not respond when you call or email her. As confusing as this may seem, it's no different than a man getting a woman's info and then never contacting her. Sometimes people change their minds or something comes up, or there wasn't ample time to establish interest or a necessary level of rapport. Don't sweat it. It's a normal part of dating, especially with women you barely know.

One of the most common questions men ask me is how many times to try contacting a woman before giving up. The answer is: once, twice at most. Often, once is enough. If a woman is truly interested, she'll respond.

If a woman is truly interested, she will respond to your call or email.

However, in some cases, a woman hasn't had a chance to get to know you well enough to know if she's interested, and sometimes it's just easier to blow it off. In this case, sometimes a second try will do the trick.

But after that, let it go. Don't keep contacting her or you'll come off desperate. And don't give her a hard time about not responding to you. A Problem Solver knows that not every girl will respond to him. Move on to the next one.

Understanding "Woman Speak"

When you ask a woman out, regardless of your mode of communication, you should get a clear yes to your request. If she hems and haws or makes excuses, she is using Woman Speak to convey that she isn't interested, or she isn't sure yet. Here are some examples of this:

"I'm kind of seeing someone..."

"I'm pretty busy right now and don't have much time to date..."

"I'm just getting out of a relationship..."

"I'm not sure I know you well enough..."

Some guys get annoyed by Woman Speak and say, "Why don't women just tell the truth?" I'll tell you why: to tell a man who has just taken a risk and asked you out, "Hey, I don't know if I like you" or, "You don't interest me, dude," is harsh. Women don't want to be harsh, and men don't like it when women are harsh.

Besides, men are no different in this way. For example, take a situation when a woman wants to proceed with a relationship but you don't. You don't say, "Hey, I don't like you" or, "I like this other chick more than you." Why? Because that would be rude! Instead, you use your own Man Speak statements, such as, "I'm not really looking to get serious right now" or, "My life is complicated right now." It's a more humane way to reject someone.

Don't worry about Woman Speak. One you learn to decode Woman Speak – and you will with time – you'll come to appreciate these excuses. If you don't get a clear "Yes," then the answer is probably "No." This doesn't mean she won't come around; some women really just aren't sure yet and need more time to decide.

If you don't get a clear "Yes," then her answer is "No."

The best way to handle this uncomfortable scenario is to back off. You can say, "Okay." Or, if you sense she's a maybe, say, "Let me know if you change your mind." If you want to be charming, smile and say, "You don't know what you're missing!" in a funny, lighthearted way. And then move on. Remember: you should never have to persuade a woman to go out with you. If she's says no, at least you had the stones to try. Kudos to you.

Example

A friend and I were chatting with a couple of men at a crowded bar during Monday Night Football. I had mentioned I was dating a guy, but that we'd only been dating 2-3 weeks. As the night wore on, and Guy #2 had more to drink, he eventually asked me out. The conversation went something like this:

Guy #2: "Can I get your phone number?"

Me: "Thanks anyway, but I'm kinda seeing someone."

Guy #2: "You've only been dating him 2-3 weeks!"

Me: Awkward shrug, "Yeah... but [some lame excuse I don't recall]..."

Because Guy #2 and I had been talking for a while, along with a good dose of "liquid courage," it makes some sense that he asked me out. Even though I said I was seeing someone, Guy #2 suspected (correctly) that the "someone" wasn't a boyfriend and that it was acceptable (albeit risky) for him to make a move.

My response indicated a Woman Speak "No." He chose to argue rather than realize that I wasn't interested.

Asking a woman out takes guts. It means facing rejection and a host of other stuff that isn't easy to handle. However, if you look for signs of interest and build rapport, your odds of getting a "yes" increase greatly. And once you do get that yes, it's time to start planning the first date.

14) THE FIRST DATE AND BEYOND

The first date is important. It establishes whether there is chemistry between the two of you, how well you interact, and whether there will be a second date. Psychologically, the first date is the beginning of a relationship, even if that relationship only lasts one evening. You will react to this in several different ways.

First, no matter how little you know your date or how unsure you are about your interest in her, you will feel some nervousness about the date. This is a natural physiological response to a new situation, much like approaching a stranger or speaking in front of a group. Most people think of nervousness as a bad thing – it isn't. It's a good thing. Why? Because studies show that humans perform best when they're a little anxious; our bodies release stress hormones that make us sharper and better able to handle the demands of the situation.[4]

Second, dating, especially early on, has a way of making you self-conscious and hyperaware of any insecurities you have. The more interested you are in a woman, the truer this is. This too is normal. A Problem Solver doesn't avoid dating, hoping these feelings will magically go away; he simply accepts these feelings and doesn't let them distract him.

This chapter will provide some guidelines to ensure that those early dates go well.

Where to Take Her

The first date should take place at a setting that is comfortable, attractive, and allows you both to get to know one another. This setting should not be fancy or expensive. The days of fancy or expensive first dates are over, and the less acquainted you are with your date, the truer this is. Why go to all that trouble and expense for a woman who may not turn out to be your type?

However, you still want to select a place that's nice, that shows you put in effort. Choose a funky, trendy, or comfortable place with good ambience. Such places make women feel good, and they'll associate that good feeling with you. If you're unsure of such a place, ask your friends or coworkers for ideas, especially if they're female.

Should you start with coffee, lunch, or dinner? It depends on where you met her and your level of acquaintance with her. The better you know her, the more likely a dinner date is appropriate. Use the table below as a guideline:

Your level of acquaintance:	First date should be:
Little to none (e.g. online dating, met briefly at a coffee shop, blind date)	Coffee, tea, or a drink
Some acquaintance (e.g. met in person and got to chat a while)	Casual lunch
Reasonably well-acquainted (e.g. a friend or coworker you know and like)	Dinner

These are not rigid rules. Do what feels right to you. In general, try to keep it simple. The focus is on getting to know one another, not what you do or where you go.

Where NOT to Take Her

No matter how little or how well you know a woman, some settings make for a poor first date experience, greatly reducing the odds that you will get a second date. These include:

- **Bars and clubs.** Even if you love bars and clubs, these places are too loud and crowded for good first date conversation. If you're meeting for a drink, pick a restaurant bar or a quiet pub. Patio bars are great in summer.

- **Parties.** Never bring a woman to a party for your first date, even if she knows the hosts. Your goal is to focus on her, not socialize with others. And never expose your new date to your friends yet. This is too much pressure for her. Save parties for when you've gotten more acquainted.

- **Weddings or family events.** Bringing a woman to a wedding or a family gathering is like bringing her to a party, only much worse. These events put too much pressure on the both of you, and take focus off getting to know her. Save these events for girlfriends.

- **Long or involved dates.** Avoid any date that will last more than an hour or two, which will already seem like a lifetime if things don't go well. Also, avoid activity dates (runs, bike rides, hikes, etc) until you get to know one another a little. Again, too much pressure.

- **Your place.** A man who invites a woman to his place for a first date comes off lazy or like he wants to get laid. It's also unsafe for women. Save this for the third date, at the earliest.

Example

Tim met Charlene on an internet dating site. Tim was a triathlete, and thus spent a lot of time riding his road bike. Charlene was interested in buying a road bike, but was a novice rider. For their first date, Tim chose to take Charlene bike riding. As a seasoned rider, Tim was in his element. But Charlene, who was trying clip-in pedals for the first time, was nervous. And she felt very self-conscious wearing tight spandex on a first date. Tim did not ask Charlene out again.

Tim made a poor choice for his first date with Charlene. Although it was generous of him to help her grow accustomed to cycling, he chose a setting where he was at ease but Charlene was far outside her comfort zone. Charlene was uncomfortable, and thus not her best self.

Other First Date Tips

If you're dating online or otherwise dating a woman you don't really know, always expect to meet her at the place where your date will take place. Never ask a woman if you can pick her up or to come to your place, for safety reasons. If you already know her, then you can offer to pick her up.

Also, until you know a woman's tastes or dietary limitations, choose restaurants that serve food and drink that is palatable to pretty much everyone. For example, choose Italian rather than Indian food. If you want to try something more interesting but are unsure if she'll like it, run it by her first. However, don't ask her for ideas or ask her to choose where to go. Women like a man who takes charge.

If you want to impress her, try a new restaurant you've heard good things about, or a favorite that your friends recommend. Opt for trendy or mom-and-pop restaurants, and avoid chains.

Who Pays?

Spring for the first date. This sends a good message to women and makes a woman feel safe, cared for, and valued. This isn't about money. After all, in this day and age, women can afford to pay for their own meal. It's a symbolic act that says, "I am a man, and I can protect and take care of you." This dating tradition has stuck around for decades for a reason – it's powerful. She may offer to chip in; just say no.

Of course, this doesn't mean you should have to pay for all dates. I teach women that after the first date or two they should offer to contribute. You aren't a sugar daddy. How much and how often you want to pay after the first date or two is your business and will depend on your attitude about such things, and your finances. It's perfectly acceptable to let a woman share the cost of dating. If you find she isn't offering after a while, you may have to talk to her about it. Say, "I wish I could afford to pay for all dates, but I can't."

If money is tight, dial down the first date. Stick with coffee or a beer. For a woman you already know (and already like), a simple lunch at a café won't set you back much. Or get some sandwiches and an inexpensive bottle of wine and go to the park.

Paying for dates is a touchy issue, and I've seen some men get very defensive about it. While some women do expect men to pay for everything, often it's men who put this pressure on themselves. One man put it perfectly:

"Plenty of guys, rightly or wrongly, are spending more than they have because they think women expect it from them. Or because they think it's the way to woo a woman."

Don't fall into this trap. If you spend money on a woman regularly, she'll assume you can and want to. A Complainer drones on about how women expect this or that; a Problem Solver knows his financial limits. Aim for fun dates, rather than expensive ones. Save the expensive stuff for women you're in love with.

Second and Third Dates

If things go well on the first date, you will probably want to ask her out again. You can do this at the end of the first date, or, to keep her guessing a little, wait to ask by calling or emailing her over the next few days. The length of time you wait before contacting her is directly proportional to your level of disinterest – i.e. the longer you wait, the less interested you are, and seem. An interested man contacts a woman within two days, three at most. Longer than that, you aren't that into her. If she responds to your call or email, ask her out again.

Once you've gotten past the first date and you feel like things are going well, you can continue with casual dating venues as you did on the first date, or, if you feel comfortable, you can plan dates that have increasing complexity, length, or cost. Move on to lunch or dinner, then to an activity you'd both enjoy. Here are a few ideas for fun second or third dates:

- Dinner and a museum
- Outdoor activity (e.g. a hike, run, bike ride, or sport you both enjoy)
- Picnic in a park
- Ball game or sporting event
- Movie and a meal, drink, or dessert
- Art walk or gallery stroll
- Festival
- Amusement park
- Cook a meal at your place (this is better for the third date or after)
- Brunch, lunch, or dinner on a nice restaurant patio
- Appetizers and drinks at a cool or funky bar

Also, when chatting with a woman on a date, listen closely – often, she will remark on places or foods she likes, giving you ideas for the next date.

If things go well with a woman you've dated a couple of times and you want to spice things up, make your next date an activity that's exciting, a little scary, or breathtaking. For example, try an amusement park with big roller coasters, a scary movie, or a hike with stunning views. Why? Research shows that emotionally arousing events together will increase the likelihood of two people becoming much closer. One caveat: make sure it's something she agrees to try. If it terrifies her, your plan will backfire.

Dating can be a lot of fun, especially when you choose activities that are conducive to building rapport and trust. Overall, no matter where you choose to go on the first few dates, focus on enjoying yourself and getting to know this woman.

15) HOW TO TALK TO WOMEN

No matter how nice the setting or how fun the activity, the centerpiece of your date is conversation. If you're good at talking to women, there's a good chance you'll get a second and third date. If, however, you make a conversational faux pas, you could be unfairly dismissed. This may seem harsh, but people are already dealing with discomfort on a date, especially a first date. If we say something that makes our date even more uncomfortable, they won't want to come back for more.

Men who have good luck with women, who attract a lot of women, know how to talk to women. Just as importantly, they know how to listen to them. While some dating experts will teach you silly tricks for conversing with women in order to generate their interest, I'm going to teach you something much more valuable: good social skills.

Social skills are people skills. They let you know what to say, how to say it, how to listen, and in general how to make others feel comfortable in your presence. On average, women have slightly better social skills than do men. This means that men need to be a bit more cautious in what they say on a date. However, like any skill, social skills can be learned, and socially skilled men have more success with women.

Socially skilled men have more success with women.

The first rule of talking to women is that you can't talk to women the same way you talk to men. This doesn't mean you need to walk on eggshells to avoid offending women, or that you need to be Mr. Sensitive. It simply means that the way to talk with men may not bring you success with women. And isn't that why you're here – to succeed with women?

If you watch a group of men talk, and then go watch a group of women talk, you will see some differences. Generally speaking, men tend to try and command the conversation and say what they need to say, until another man jumps in, takes over, and does the same. They may boast, tell jokes, talk trash, or poke fun at one another. Some men are very much this way, and others less so, but these tendencies are there. Women, on the other hand, while they too want to be heard, are just as concerned with making sure the others get heard. They don't talk over one another as much, and are more supportive. They rarely boast, tell jokes, talk trash, or make fun of one another. In fact, doing any of those things can cause a woman to be quickly ousted from the group.

These differences are okay. Both styles have their place. However, if you want to win a woman over, it helps to talk to her in the style she's accustomed to. You don't need to do this for the entire date, only enough to make her feel comfortable. In other words, when out on a date, you'll need to shift gears a bit.

Tips for Talking to a Woman on a Date

Here are some ways you can shift into "date conversation" when out with a woman to increase your odds of success with her.

Don't Take Over the Conversation

One of the top complaints I get from single women is that they went out on a date with a man and he did nothing but talk about himself the entire time. Sure, a woman will let you go on and on about that year you spent in Tibet, including your service in their army and an ascent up Mt. Everest. Hell, she may even appear interested after forty minutes have passed. She isn't. She's being polite. If you're a talker or a storyteller, resist the temptation to go on too long. The problem isn't the stories; it's going on far too long without including her in the conversation. Tell your story and then ask her about herself. If she's quiet or introverted, it's okay to do more of the talking, just don't do ALL the talking.

Why do men do this? Usually, because they're nervous or because they want to impress a woman. However, while it's nice to impress her, your main job is to get to know her, and for her to get to know you. Women enjoy being entertained, but what they really want is to connect. Connection won't happen if you don't include her in the conversation.

Women enjoy being entertained, but they prefer to connect.

If you focus on entertaining or impressing a woman, you may accomplish both, but you may not hear from her again.

Example

One way to avoid connecting with a woman in conversation is to drone on about a story without including her. Take this example:

Her: What did you do last weekend?

Him: I was in Breckenridge, skiing. It was great. The snow was perfect. (Goes on for a while about his ski trip). It was a bit cold, though. It got down close to 10 degrees. My ears were killing me...

Her: Oh, I totally know how that feels. That happened to me last year, and I actually wound up with a bit of frostbite on my ear.

Him: Uh huh. So, I went into the lodge and got a new hat... (Goes on with story).

What happened? She asked him about himself and he had an interesting answer, which is good. But his story got a bit long, so she chimed in. This was her attempt to be included in the conversation. He ignored her attempt and kept telling the story, as if that were the main goal. The story is never the main goal; connecting with her is. Instead, he should have acknowledged what she said before resuming his story. For example, when she mentioned frostbite, he'd say, "Really? Is it okay?" She would nod yes and show him the scar, and then he would continue with the rest of his story. After, he might then ask her if she skis, or what she did last weekend. Connect, don't entertain.

Ask Her about Herself

If you want to win a woman over, show genuine interest in what she has to say by asking questions. Ask her about her job, her hobbies, or her travels. If you find that she is particularly interested in one topic, ask her more about that. Most of all, ask – don't wait for her to volunteer the information. This shows genuine interest, and excellent social skill.

Be sure, however, to avoid interrogating. Never ask a woman too many questions in row or put her on the spot with difficult questions. Instead, encourage her to talk, then you can chime in or talk about your own experiences.

Listen Without Interrupting

When talking to a woman, let her say what she needs to say and rein in any temptation to jump in, take over, or not let her finish. Interrupting basically says, "What you're saying is less important than what I have to say." An occasional interruption is okay, especially if you have a pertinent comment or question. However, if you do interrupt, be sure to acknowledge that you did and encourage her to resume what she was saying.

Nod or Acknowledge

A good listener listens, but a really good listener responds to a woman's commentary with an occasional nod, acknowledgement, or a brief one-word comment such as "hmmm" or "interesting." This shows you're interested in what she has to say, rather than simply waiting until it's your turn to speak.

Ignore Mistakes

If a woman makes a grammatical mistake or another type of conversational error, don't correct her. Experts say that over-looking people's gaffes is the way to charm them, especially if they're aware they made the gaffe.[5]

Even if you comment, don't correct a woman. I once had a guy, after I ordered my drink from the bartender, say, "Please." He corrected me by telling me I should say "please" after politely ordering my drink. This is rude and unnecessary. If you find that a woman's grammar is incorrect or her manners lacking, simply ignore it or don't ask her out again. To correct a woman is arrogant. She's your date, not your child or student.

Don't Criticize What She Likes (Even if You Hate It)

If a woman says she loves Coldplay and you hate them, don't say, "How can you like them? They suck." When you do this, you effectively say, "You suck." To criticize her taste is to criticize her. This doesn't mean you have to pretend to like Coldplay. Simply say nothing, and if she asks, you say, "Yeah, I admit Coldplay isn't my favorite." This effectively says, "I don't like them, but it's fine if you do." This general principle will serve you in all areas of life. People take everything personally, and if you criticize what they like, they won't like you.

Acknowledge Her Opinions

While the first few dates aren't a time for bringing up controversial topics, you may still stumble upon something you both disagree on. Men who are successful with women acknowledge a woman's opinion. This does not mean you have to agree with her or squelch your own opinions. You don't. It means sticking to your opinions without judging hers or trying to convince her she's wrong. A confident man is comfortable in his opinions. He does not engage in debates or pissing contests with women to determine who's "right." If he does, he may win the battle, but he'll lose the woman.

Instead, express your point of view, then listen to hers. This is especially important if you're an opinionated guy who loves debate or enjoys being right. Practice saying, "Good point" or, "Interesting" or, "I never thought of it that way." This makes her feel listened to, acknowledged, and respected, but doesn't mean you lose ground or compromise yourself. If you find that you strongly disagree with something she says, then say so, but don't judge her for her opinion.

In the same vein, you want to avoid competing with a woman you're dating, whether it's for who's right or who's the faster runner. To compete with a woman and attempt to "win" shows insecurity, not confidence. And it's a huge turnoff. A confident man doesn't have to prove anything to a woman or to anyone else – he knows what he has going for him.

Watch Your Humor

Men often poke fun at one another or use crude humor. But you have to be very cautious about doing so with women. Avoid this until you and she become comfortable around one another. Even then, *never* make fun of a woman's body or looks, or anything she's sensitive about.

Find Common Ground

Above, I said that women want to connect in a conversation. Socially skilled people connect by finding common ground with those they're speaking to. During conversation, look for things that resonate with both of you – a common experience, interest, opinion, or fascination. You will know when it happens.

When you talk to women you date, whether they're demure and sweet or tough and successful, they want to feel heard and respected. This is how you succeed with women. Review the points I made above now and again. You will find that they'll serve you not only in dating, but in many areas of life.

16) AVOIDING THE TOP 10 DATING BLUNDERS

If you're out on a date with a woman, you've already done a lot of the hard work and achieved much success. Thus, it's important to avoid sabotaging that success by making dating blunders that can diminish a woman's interest in you. As I've said, the early stages of dating are uncomfortable for many people. Women who aren't aware that this is normal may unconsciously look for reasons to escape this discomfort. Don't give her any.

Many dating blunders can be avoided with good social skills, as I discussed in the previous chapter. However, there are certain no-no's when it comes to dating. Fortunately, with a few simple guidelines, you can avoid them.

The Top 10 Dating Blunders

Although there are lots of things that can go wrong on a date, most aren't a big deal. However, there are some things that are almost guaranteed to derail a date. This section discusses the 10 most common ones.

Dating Blunder #1: Talking About Your Ex

It's a huge turnoff for a woman to have to hear about your ex on a date. It doesn't matter whether you say good things, bad things, or neutral things. Talking about her tells your date that your ex is still on your mind. Not a good sign. It also takes the focus off of her, off the two of you, and off the present. Never mention your ex on a date, even briefly.

If you have children, your ex is a permanent part of your life, for better or for worse. Still, avoid mentioning her. If you must mention her, for example to tell her you dropped the kids off at her house earlier, refer to her as "the kids' mom." This sounds much better than "my ex." If a woman asks you about her, keep your answer very neutral and very brief.

Dating Blunder #2: Talking About Previous Relationships

Never bring up past relationships on early dates. This makes many women uncomfortable. Talking about your previous relationships – what worked, what didn't work, what you learned, or anything else – is much like talking about your ex. It puts focus on the past and your previous life, and takes focus off your date, the present, and your potential future life. Remember: this is a date, not a therapy session.

You will find, however, that some women will talk about their past relationships, or will encourage you to. Don't fall for it. It will greatly decrease the odds of getting another date because the risk of saying the wrong thing or saying too much is too great. The best way to handle an inquiry about your past relationships is to say, "That's an important question. But maybe we should wait until we get to know one another better before opening up the Ex Files." This shows you aren't evading, but simply being appropriate. Say it with humor. She'll get the point.

Dating Blunder #3: Talking About Your Divorce

Some divorced men, especially if dating a divorced woman, are prone to talking about their divorces on dates. This is especially true if the divorce is recent or has not been finalized yet. It's perfectly acceptable to reveal that you're divorced, and you should definitely mention if you're still getting divorced. However, leave it at that.

Divorce has a very strong impact on those who've been through it, and it can teach you a lot. It's tempting to talk about it and what you learned from it. However, this kind of discussion is a slippery slope, and you can wind up saying the wrong things, saying too much, or talking about the ex, all of which can sabotage a perfectly good date. Save it. If you and she hit it off, you'll have plenty of time to swap divorce stories.

Dating Blunder #4: Mentioning Sex

Never mention sex, make sexual innuendos, or make any reference to sex when on the first few dates. Although every woman is different when it comes to this, you don't know how she feels about discussing such things yet, nor do you know if she's attracted to you yet. The more she finds it uncomfortable to discuss sexual topics with someone she hardly knows, and the less sure she is of her attraction to you, the more bringing up sex will backfire, big time.

Wait until you and she are comfortable with one another and you feel confident there is mutual attraction. This can take at least a few dates, even longer.

Dating Blunder #5: Discussing Health Problems

Health problems can include any significant issue with your physical or mental health. A health problem is one of those things that most people are fine with if they know you, but will scare them if they don't know you. Thus, never bring this up on a first date.

There is a psychological sweet spot for discussing health problems with a woman. That sweet spot is somewhere between the third and sixth date – after you and she have become comfortable with one another but before things get serious. This way, a woman can evaluate the reality you're dealing with, in the context of knowing and liking you. If you speak too soon, you may scare her off or reveal something personal to an unworthy person. If you wait too long, you will be too attached to one another before you know if your relationship can handle your challenge. The more serious the problem, the truer this is.

Dating Blunder #6: Negativity

Nothing kills a date faster than negativity. Examples of negativity include complaining about the service in a restaurant, complaining about dating, badmouthing your ex, or expressing disgust with the economy. Negativity not only ruins the mood on a date, which should be fun and positive, it also makes you look like someone who will be a drag to be with.

If something goes wrong on the date (e.g. it takes an hour to get your meals), briefly acknowledge the problem and, if necessary, make a suggestion for a solution. Don't complain or let it ruin the date. Remember: a Problem Solver doesn't complain; he focuses on how to fix it.

If you have a tendency to be negative, cynical, or critical, you will struggle in dating and relationships. Try to keep them at bay when dating; but also, take a hard look at yourself and remember that negativity and cynicism are choices you make every day. They don't reflect the world; they reflect your view of it.

Dating Blunder #7: Forgetting to be a Gentleman

On a date, be sure to be thoughtful. Open doors for your date. Let her order first. If she meets you at a bar or coffee joint, offer to get her something. Listen without interrupting. Keep your phone turned off and out of view. If you know her well enough, offer to pick her up at her home. When you drop her off, wait until you know she's safe in her home before you drive away. If you meet her, offer to walk her to her car, especially if it's dark out. If she drove in bad weather, text her to make sure she got home okay.

You should also be considerate when a woman comes to your home. Offer her something to drink. Give her a tour. Keep your dog from humping her leg or jumping on her nice outfit. Make her feel comfortable in your home.

If you bring her to a party or a function where she doesn't know people or doesn't know them well (NOT your first date, of course), make sure you introduce her to people. Do not ignore her while you socialize with your friends.

Remember: chivalry is an easy and cost-free way to really impress a woman.

Chivalry is an easy and cost-free way to impress a woman.

Dating Blunder #8: Asking Personal Questions

There are some questions that are too personal to ask in the first few dates. Some examples of these include:

"What led up to your getting divorced?"

"Why did your past relationships end?"

"What kind of relationship are you looking for?"

"Are you looking to have kids?"

"What are your goals in life?"

When you ask these questions, you put your date in the uncomfortable position of either having to answer something too personal too soon, or having to tell you it's too personal to answer right now. Such questions have no business on the first date, and should be avoided until you're better acquainted.

There are also some questions that should never be asked. These include:

"Why are you still single?"

"Why don't you have kids?"

There is no good answer to these questions. The first question is insulting and insinuates that being single is a problem. If you're concerned that a woman has been single for years or hasn't married by the age of 45, date her – the reasons will reveal themselves, but they may be reasons you can live with. The second question is too personal and comes off sounding like not having kids is bad. Women who don't have kids either still want them, have decided not to have them, or cannot have them. Again, with time, you'll find out which one it is.

People who ask personal questions are often trying to "test" their date to avoid winding up with the wrong person. This is the wrong way to go about it. When you get too personal, you come off inappropriate or like you're interrogating. You may rule out the wrong ones; but you will also rule out the right ones. Instead, listen. Often, women will reveal who they are on their own.

Dating Blunder #9: Drinking Too Much

Never drink more than two drinks on dates 1-3. I don't care if you're Canadian or weigh 250 lbs. Drinking more than this lowers your inhibitions, putting you at risk for making any of the other dating blunders and a variety of other mistakes. If you picked up your date, it also means putting her at risk when you drive her home. Plus, while you may not notice, your date will notice you stumble or slur your words, making you appear less attractive.

Dating Blunder #10: Talking Too Much

I already talked about this in the previous chapter, but it bears mentioning again, especially since it's such a common complaint. Remember, it's okay to impress her, but you also want to connect with her. Always include her in the conversation.

When you examine the Top 10 dating blunders, many of them revolve around TMI, or Too Much Information. Often, people reveal TMI in an attempt to create intimacy or connection with a date. But creating a connection cannot be rushed, and is better accomplished by connecting over less serious topics.

A Complainer might say, "I just want to be myself on a date. And if my dates don't like what I have to say, then to hell with them." You're welcome to do things "your way" – but wouldn't you rather do what works? A Problem Solver does what works, while still being himself. If his TMI doesn't get him the girls he wants, he learns why such things make women uncomfortable, and avoids doing them.

Alternatively, you may say, "Wait. In my experience, it's the *women* who get too personal too soon." Yes, women dig getting personal, and are probably more prone to TMI than men. However, men aren't immune. Men who are comfortable talking about personal stuff, and men who have been through a lot of personal stuff (e.g. a divorce), tend to want to talk about it. They don't always feel comfortable talking to men, so they talk to women, knowing that women love talking about relationships and other personal stuff. This is okay – just don't do it too soon or get carried away.

"So What SHOULD I Talk About?"

Now that you know what to avoid on a date, you can focus on having fun and getting to know her. On the first few dates, and especially the first date, stick to topics that are less personal, free of controversy, and positive or fun. It's perfectly acceptable to talk about work or your profession, your hobbies, pets, TV and movies, how you spent last weekend, where you've traveled, where you want to travel, your passions. Keep the discussion lightweight. Once you bond over those topics, with time you will naturally broach deeper ones.

Overall, don't worry if you've made any of the Top 10 dating blunders. We all have. It's part of the learning experience. A Problem Solver simply corrects his mistakes and keeps going.

17) DATING OLDER WOMEN

In this day and age, more and more men are dating older women. Since 1960, marriages where the man is older have decreased, and marriages where the wife is older have increased.[6] There are many reasons for this. For one, social and economic changes in our society have made it so women are no longer dependent upon men to support them. Also, there are fewer expectations to follow the traditional "fall in love, get married, have kids, stay married forever" model. Without these constraints, men and women are free to venture outside of convention.

However, while dating an older woman has become more common, doing so is still somewhat outside the norm. And doing anything outside the norm has a psychology all its own. This chapter will discuss the issues around dating an older woman, and offer you advice on how to do so successfully. Also, while this chapter is useful for dating any woman who is older than you, it is especially useful when dating women 10 or more years older than you.

Why Older Women?

Men who date or get involved with older women usually fall into one of two categories:

1) Cougar Chasers

2) Men who date older women

Cougar Chasers

These days, there are about 100 definitions of "Cougar," ranging from a much older woman who voraciously preys upon men half her age for sex, to any woman who is older than you are. The real definition is between these extremes: a Cougar is a woman who intentionally dates significantly younger men, usually with the goal of NSA or casual dating.

Cougar Chasers target Cougars because they have good reason to believe a Cougar will share their relationship goals – i.e. a desire for NSA or casual dating. Some people believe that Cougar Chasers are the only kind of men who date older women. That is not the case.

Men Who Date Older Women

There are many men who date, get involved with, or marry older women. Some of these men prefer older women, perhaps because they're drawn to their maturity or to some other trait that's harder to find in a younger woman. More often, a man who dates an older woman didn't necessarily seek her out intentionally. Instead, he dated a variety of women and ended up hitting it off with one who was older.

From the perspective of the two C's – chemistry and compatibility – these men feel chemistry for the older woman, but happen to find a greater level of compatibility with an older woman.

The Benefits of Dating Older Women

When I've spoken with men who've dated older women and asked them what they like about dating them, many of them say the same things. Here they are:

They're more confident. Older women are often more confident and comfortable in their own skin. They've overcome challenges and faced their insecurities. And older women are often much more comfortable asking for what they want instead of hoping someone (i.e. you) will give it to them. Men find this confidence sexy, and they like knowing where a woman stands instead of trying to read her mind.

There's less drama. All women have their ups and downs, but older women are usually better at navigating them because they've learned to understand themselves. They're also more likely to have learned to deal with conflict in constructive way.

They're more independent. Many older women have learned to take care of themselves instead of expecting men to. This is true financially as well as emotionally. Older women are more likely to have well-paying jobs, satisfying careers, and a full life. All of this means less pressure on you.

They're sexually experienced. Older women, who've had more relationships or longer relationships, are more experienced in bed. They're also more likely to ask for what they want and to be far more comfortable in their sexuality than younger women. Some have stronger sex drives than they did when younger. This means better sex for you.

They've been there, done that. By the time a woman reaches her 40s, she's probably already been married and had kids. Or, she's realized marriage and/or kids aren't that important to her. If you aren't really into the idea of getting married or having kids, an older woman may be a good option for you.

Again, these are traits men have said they like about the older women they've dated. This does not mean all older women have these traits, so you have to weigh each one individually, just as you would any woman.

Concerns about Dating Older Women

Many men have some concerns about dating older women, especially if the age difference is significant. I discuss each of these concerns below:

"Older women don't want men my age." This is a Complainer's mindset. True, some older women are that way, but many aren't, especially if they feel some type of chemistry with you. This is the case with any woman of any age – some will be game, and some won't. A Problem Solver utilizes the techniques I discuss in Chapters 10 and 12; if he doesn't get a date, he moves on.

You want kids. Some men, in the hopes that they will someday have kids, get nervous about dating women over 40. If you are totally dead set on having kids, then stick with women 40ish or younger. However, if you are on the fence about kids, or you are over 40 yourself, I urge you to consider women over 40. You don't want to rule out a potentially good thing with a woman to hold out for something that isn't a high priority for you.

Example

About four years ago, Neal, an acquaintance of mine and a good guy, dated a woman who was older than him. He was close to 40, and she was 48. He really liked her; she was sophisticated, smart, and they got along well. However, Neal ended things with this woman. When I asked him why, he said that even though he wasn't sure he wanted kids, he "didn't want to rule out the possibility of kids." Currently, Neal still has no kids. In fact, he's still single.

While there is no guarantee things would have worked out with this woman, Neal's choice to focus on younger women for the sake of possibly having kids has not served him. Kids are not a high priority for him, so he should focus on women he's compatible with and stop worrying about age.

"What will she look like when she's 50??" Even if you recognize that older women can be very attractive, both physically and otherwise, you may still worry about the aging process. If you're

35 and dating a 48-year-old, you may wonder, "What will she look like when I'm 45 and she's 58?" That is something to consider if the age difference between you is quite large, such as 15 years or greater.

However, regardless of the age difference, remember that while she is aging, so are you, and at the same rate. If she takes care of herself now, she probably will when she's older too. And if you find that you have a very strong connection and a high level of compatibility with an older woman, you will remain attracted to her regardless of her age. This has been the experience of men who have embarked on long term relationships with much older women. The connection keeps them together because it's based on more than physical chemistry.

In the end, if a Problem Solver has concerns about dating an older woman, he doesn't give up; he gets answers.

Guidelines for Dating Older Women

In many ways, dating an older woman is no different than dating one your age. However, on some level, when dating an older woman you face a couple of minor challenges from a psychology standpoint. One is a slight power differential – in a relationship with an age difference, the older person is generally wiser and more knowledgeable than the younger one. The other is the going-against-the-norm thing. These factors can create problems; the greater the age difference, the truer this is. However, with some awareness of the following, you can avoid these problems.

Don't be intimidated. Many men have admitted to me that they're more intimidated by an older woman than a younger one. The more attractive and accomplished she is, the more intimidating she may seem. However, while you may wonder what she sees in you when she could date more accomplished men her age, she may wonder what you see in her when you could date younger women. Deep down, behind her confidence, she's just a woman who wants to be appreciated. Be your confident self with her.

Take the lead. No matter how much older and more accomplished she is than you, you still need to take the lead when you date an older woman. Get her digits, ask her out, and decide on where to take her. Regardless of her age or success, she's still a woman and women like men who handle things. Taking the lead will project confidence and impress her. By contrast, letting her take the lead can cause her to feel like your mother. Not good.

Pay your way. The same rules for paying apply with an older woman, even if she makes three times your income. Spring for the first date, then let her chip in after that. Don't feel you have to outspend yourself to impress her; effort matters more than cash. She knows she makes more than you and doesn't care. Never let her buy you things or take care of you – this disrupts the equality of the relationship and puts you into gold-digger/sugar-mama territory.

Don't joke about her age. Older women are often more comfortable with themselves, including their age, than younger women. But society still denigrates older women and women can be touchy about age, so it's a bad idea to make age-related jokes. However, age doesn't have to be a taboo subject; after all, the bigger the age difference, the more useful it may be to discuss any issues.

Avoid asking for advice too often. If a woman is older than you, she may be more experienced and/or wiser in certain areas. Don't look to her for advice, as this sets up a mother-son dynamic. Likewise, if she's the mothering type or feels the need to guide you or tell you what to do, don't let her get away with it. Remember: no matter how large the age difference, relationships only work when the partners are equals. Share your concerns, but do your own thing. She'll respect you for it.

Example

Patricia (38) dated Shawn (32) for several months. Patricia had an established career, but Shawn was still struggling with his. He was looking for full-time work in his area of expertise, but the job search was very challenging for him, requiring lots of interviews, tests, paperwork, and travel. Shawn often stressed out about the job search process, especially the testing. Patricia, who used to work in the corporate world, tried encouraging Shawn, giving him perspective on what companies look for with those tests.

However, during their time together, Shawn talked a lot about his worries, complained about the process, and began soliciting Patricia's advice. Patricia wanted to see Shawn succeed, but she grew tired of feeling like his advisor. To her, the way Shawn handled his situation made him seem immature, younger than 32. Their relationship did not last.

It was good that Shawn felt comfortable sharing his struggles with Patricia. However, he went too far and leaned on her too much, which made her feel compelled to advise him. This became a drain on them, and disrupted the equality between them.

Don't worry about what your friends think. If you date an older woman, expect your friends to give you a hard time, at least at first. The ribbing will usually stop once they get to know her. If you find her attractive, they probably will too. And when they see that she gets along with you, treats you well, and treats them well, they'll back off and forget about the age difference.

Don't let Mom interfere. Strangely, in some cases, the person who provides the biggest barrier in younger man-older woman relationships is the man's mother. If your mother expresses disapproval of your dating an older woman, listen to her concerns, but make your own choice. Never let Mom dictate your life or talk down to your girlfriend.

Whether you're a Cougar Chaser or just a guy who's open to dating older women, you can succeed with an older woman if you know exactly what kind of relationship you want and approach the older woman with confidence. I've met many men who found what they were looking for with an older woman.

In the end, it doesn't matter how old your partner is. What matters is that you're happy. And, sometimes, happiness comes in a package you don't expect.

18) DATING WOMEN WITH KIDS

In this day and age, with the current divorce rate, the odds of dating a single mom are higher than ever. As you may have guessed, dating a single mom is different than dating a woman with no kids. Unlike childless women, a single mom has something that utilizes a significant portion of her time, energy, and love. And while some men find this daunting, others have found that it's worth it for the right girl.

There are several important issues to consider when dating a single mom. This chapter discusses the pros of the single mom, and how to date one successfully.

Why Single Moms?

For some men, a single mom's priorities and lifestyle suit them. Single moms have pros that can give them an advantage over women without kids. These pros include:

Less pressure for you. If you aren't sure about having kids or about marriage, consider dating a single mom. This is true whether or not you've already had your own kids. A single mom, while potentially willing to have more kids, usually doesn't need to have them because she's already done so. This can take a lot of heat off of you. In addition, single moms are often less intent on marriage, because, in most cases, they've already done that too. Finally, a single mom is less likely to expect constant attention from you because she's busy, giving you freedom to do your thing.

A single mom can be a good choice for men who don't want kids.

Kids can be fun. If you enjoy being around kids, dating a single mom allows you to do a lot of things you probably haven't done since you were a kid yourself. Kids give you an excuse to go to amusement parks, museums, zoos, beaches, swimming pools, batting cages, Go-carts, funny movies, and all kinds of fun stuff most adults rarely get to do. And, you get to do these things without the greater burden of raising your own kids. Kids have a zest for life and a sweet innocence lacking in adults, and they can be a real inspiration.

More maturity. Being a parent means that a woman is typically mature and knows how to care for others and get things done. You're less likely to see a single mom spending tons of money on clothes or getting drunk every weekend. In general, parents learn to think about what's best for their kids, and their partners, rather than just themselves.

A chance to be a role model. If a relationship with a single mom gets serious, you have an opportunity to be a good role model to a child. If the kids are fortunate enough to have a kind dad who's available to them, you can still offer something he can't – perhaps you're a good mountain biker and he isn't, and you can teach them that. And if the kids' dad is not around much, not a nice guy, or has disappeared altogether, your influence as a good guy who cares can have a HUGE influence on their development. Even if the relationship doesn't work out, your positive influence on those kids will never be forgotten.

"Won't I Always Come in Second Place?"

On the other hand, one of the biggest concerns men have shared with me regarding dating a single mom is the fear that they will always come in second place to the kids. It's perfectly natural to not want to come in second, third, or fourth in someone's life. You don't want to feel like you're less important than children, just as women don't want to feel less important than your job or your friends.

To some extent, this worry is understandable, as single moms are more likely to dote on their kids than are single dads. This is part biology, part societal expectations. However, with many single moms, this worry is unfounded. Most have good boundaries with their kids and have room for a man in their life. And keep in mind that all kids get more independent as they get older, and eventually move out on their own, freeing up her time to be with you.

During the dating phase, you will take second (or lower) place with a single mom. That's exactly how it ought to be – she doesn't know you well and should never make you more important than her own priorities. But over time, once things get serious with her, your priority should begin to rise. By the time you move in together or marry, you should be on an equal plane with the kids. No second place. Male or female, it's a parent's job to take care of kids, not to make them more important than their partners.

Every Single Mom is Different

It's easy to make generalizations about single moms. But they're all different. Each situation is different, and you'll find that some are very compatible with your needs, while others are not. Here are a few things to evaluate when you meet a single mom you like:

The Kids

How many kids does she have? How old are they? More kids mean more challenges and that she's busier. Younger kids require much more time and effort, but they also tend to be sweeter and more accepting of new people (like you). She may also have kids in college or fully mature kids, which frees up a lot of her time.

Custody and Parenting Time

Custody refers to who makes the decisions that affect how the child is raised, including where they go to school, what religion they're raised with, etc. She may have full custody, or share it with

Dad, where such decisions are made jointly. Shared custody is a good thing; however, if she has a conflicted relationship with her ex, there may be arguments, even court battles, over what's best for the kids.

Parenting time refers to how much time the kids spend with each parent, regardless of custody. Some single moms have their kids full time because Dad bailed out or because he lives in another state or country. This is a lot more work for her, which will affect how much time she has with you. Other single moms share parenting time with Dad; usually, Mom gets at least 50% time (often more), but this setup gives her more free time while the kids are at Dad's house.

Parenting Style

Some moms are very strict with kids, others are quite lenient. Some dote on their children and seem to live for them, others are more independent and expect their kids to be too. A Complainer might go on about how a woman mishandles her kids and then assume all single moms are the same. A Problem Solver would just move on to a new woman who handles her kids in a way he finds appropriate. Overall, some parenting styles will jive with you, and others won't.

Also, pay attention to what kind of boundaries she has. Boundaries are important for establishing what's acceptable for the kids, and what is not. Some moms allow their kids to come into her bedroom, even sleep in her bed; others require kids to knock first and to sleep in their own beds. Some moms are available for their children 24/7 (including during dates), even if it isn't important, whereas other moms let Dad or the babysitter handle it unless it's an emergency. Since there is little point in telling a single mom how to parent her children, simply find one whose style fits your comfort level.

Guidelines for Dating a Single Mom

If you do meet a single mom you like, here are a few guidelines to ensure that things go successfully with her:

Be Aware of her Priorities

No matter how important you are to a single mom, she's still got a lot on her plate. She has a job and the same responsibilities you have, but she also has to care for her kids (or get a babysitter), help with homework, cook, clean, discipline, get them to and from school, deal with their father, and handle any unexpected problems that come up. Sometimes these things will take precedence over you. This doesn't mean these things are more important than you; they're just part of being a parent.

Be Flexible

Dating a woman with kids means dealing with the unexpected. Sometimes kids get sick or have issues a mom must attend to, or visitation with Dad can suddenly change. This may occasionally upset plans you have with her. If it's unavoidable, a Problem Solver just rolls with it. However, it is not acceptable for her to interrupt your dates or time together every time her kid wants her attention or gets upset over something small. A good parent has good boundaries.

Take Your Time with the Kids

It's a good sign if a single mom wants you to meet her kids. Most women don't introduce their kids to a man until she's serious about him. However, some women are very casual about this and will let you meet the kids right off the bat. Decide whether or not you feel comfortable with this. If you don't, you can request to put off meeting them until you get to know her better.

When you meet her kids, don't be alarmed if they don't warm up to you right away. This isn't unusual, and with time they should grow to like you. Don't try to force yourself on them, and avoid trying to "buy" them with lots of gifts or toys. Just give them some space, be nice, and let them learn to like you.

If you do meet the kids, avoid getting too attached to them or investing a lot in them until you feel sure that the relationship is going somewhere. While all relationships involve risk, you don't want to give your all to a woman's kids unless you feel it's worth the risk.

Let Her Handle the Discipline

If a woman's kid acts up, let her handle it. If she doesn't handle it or you disagree with how she does, discuss it in private and avoid being critical. Everyone has a different parenting style, and you want to date a single mom who shares yours. Otherwise, you're in for a miserable ride.

> *Example*
>
> Holden met Jana, a single mom, online. They began dating and, with time, Holden met Jana's 7-year-old son, Ben. When out at a restaurant, Ben did not say please and thank you, so Holden took it upon himself to correct Ben's behavior. Holden's attitude was, "These kids need to learn their manners, and I'm not going to sit back and say nothing."

Holden was out of line. It's not his place to discipline someone else's children. Instead, he should have talked about his concerns with Jana. In this case, his talking to her probably wouldn't have helped. Holden's discipline style was too different from Jana's. They were not compatible.

Pamper Her

All women love when men do nice things for them. However, a single mom's idea of "nice" may differ from other women. Parenting is very rewarding, but it's also tiring and unromantic, leaving the single mom starved for someone to take care of her for a change. If things are going well and you want to win her over, give her what she cannot (or will not) give herself. Some ideas include giving her a massage, cooking her a meal, or offering to pay for a babysitter, which ensures you some alone time with her. For a gift, consider giving her a gift certificate for a pedicure or day spa, or hiring someone to clean her home. Every woman is different, so you'll have to gauge which gifts mean the most to her.

Look For Red Flags

As I mentioned earlier, every single mom is different, so it's important to date one whose situation jives with your needs. Beyond that, however, there are some Red Flags to be on the lookout for when dating a single mom:

- You've been dating quite a while, and she excludes you from activities involving the kids
- Her kids are often poorly behaved, or she lets them treat you poorly
- She often interrupts your dates for unimportant kid issues
- She's so busy that she never makes you a priority
- She wants you to babysit or parent for her, even though you haven't been dating long

Be Cool to Dad

Most kids have a dad out there somewhere. And there may come a time when you will meet him. Fortunately for you, baby daddies are generally easier to deal with than baby mamas are for women. Be respectful to him. Never step on his toes by trying to prove you're a better role model, even if you are. If he's a difficult man, she needs to deal with him. Support her, but don't try to fix it or fight her battles.

Single moms can come with certain challenges, but they also come with rewards you may not get with childless women. Most men find that the challenges are worth it for the right woman. And, as you can see from this chapter, single moms come in all varieties. A Problem Solver doesn't run for the hills when he meets a single mom, afraid that a child will ruin the romance. Instead, he finds out her situation, gets to know her, and sees if she's a good fit for his needs.

SUCCESS
AND ONLINE
DATING

19) KNOWING WHAT TO EXPECT

Online dating used to be something many people felt embar-rassed to admit they were doing. Those days are over. Millions of singles are logging in and meeting new people this way. However, if you're used to dating conventionally, online dating is whole new ballgame. And, online dating has a complex psychology all its own.

Often, when someone who hasn't dated online before finally decides to give it a whirl, they approach the task with a certain amount of assumptions and expectations, many of which are based on conventional dating. And, while some people enjoy online dating, many find it frustrating or give up altogether. Why is this?

Because they have unrealistic expectations.

This makes sense – after dating conventionally for so many years, you've learned what to expect and you know the drill. Online dating is a new drill, so the first step to succeeding at it, and meeting some great women, is to adjust your expectations.

Most frustration with online dating comes from unrealistic expectations.

Below, I discuss some things you should know about dating online. Once you have an idea of what to expect, the learning experience will be easier.

(The Illusion of) Endless Options

One of the great things about dating online is the sheer number of single women looking to date. Thus, it's natural to feel like there are so many women to choose from. And while, yes, online dating does expand your potential pool of women and allow you to meet women you wouldn't normally meet, the belief that there are tons of women to choose from can, ironically, limit you.

Because a given dating site will have thousands, even millions of women on it, it can feel like there are endless choices. And when humans are given endless choices, they tend to have a more difficult time choosing. As such, some men will pass over women who could be good matches for them in the search for someone "better" or more interesting. And, studies have shown that when dating online, people are often much pickier than they are when dating conventionally.

For example, given that there are tons of women online, it may be tempting to overlook an attractive woman who seems interesting merely because she's two years older or two inches shorter than your ideal. After all, with that many women, you might as well target your ideal, right? In reality, while there are lots of available women online, most of them aren't available to YOU. I expand on why this is in the "dating is a numbers game" section below.

What does this mean for you? It means that while, yes, dating online will increase your options, the options are not endless and the actual pool of women you will meet is not nearly as huge as it may appear. It's important to avoid being too picky or dismissive, and to focus on meeting quality women.

A Profile Differs From a Real Person

In conventional dating, you know you're interested in a woman, so you take her out. But in online dating, things work in the reverse – you go out with a woman to see if you're interested. A woman may look attractive in her photo and seem interesting in her profile, but all that can change in an instant when you meet in person. And until you meet in person, interest isn't real.

Women are not always like their profiles. Sometimes this is because they're deceptive – e.g. they post photos that differ from what they look like in person, or they come off friendly and interesting when in fact they aren't either. However, more often, a woman may seem different in person because her photo and write-up only give you a one-dimensional "snapshot" of who she is, whereas a woman you meet in person is three-dimensional and far more complex.

Thus, it's important to remember this, and to keep an open mind, when you date online.

Your Profile Matters. A Lot.

A good profile is extremely important if you want to increase your options with women online. Unfortunately, many men see how easy it is sign up on a dating site and to toss up a quick profile, under the assumption that will be enough to get dates.

It isn't.

A sloppily written profile with a low-quality photo from two years ago will get you in the game, but it won't get you the results you want. Remember: online, all you are to a woman is a photo and write-up, among a sea of other men. If you don't stand out, you won't find what you're looking for.

Online Dating is Uncomfortable

Online dating involves meeting and interacting with women who are complete strangers. Even if this sounds fun and adventurous to you – and it doesn't for many men – dealing with strangers will have some awkward moments. The truth is, humans don't trust strangers, especially strangers they've never met. Moreover, women don't usually trust strange men. You may be harmless, but some other men online aren't.

Thus, dating online can be uncomfortable, more uncomfortable than conventional dating. Some people, when they meet someone online, expect to achieve an instant connection, to have instantaneous rapport, or to feel immediate chemistry. This is unrealistic. Others hope to hide the awkward nature of interacting with strangers. There is no need. If you feel awkward about it, or notice that the women you meet seem uncomfortable, that's not unusual. Instead of fighting it, embrace it. With patience, the awkwardness will go away.

Online Dating is a Numbers Game

When you date online, your yield in terms of successful dates is much lower than in conventional dating. Good prospects may turn into nothing. You may chat with women and get no date out of it. You may go out on a lot of first "dates" that never turn into second dates. They may not be what you're looking for, you may not be what they're looking for, or the chemistry just isn't there. You may have to weed through a lot of women before you find someone you click with. Some men struggle with this because they're used to conventional dating, where you usually know up front if there's mutual interest.

Also, although some women will contact you first, you will have to initiate most of the contact with women online. Of those you contact, there will be many who say they aren't interested, and many others who never reply at all. If you do get emails from women, some will bear no resemblance to the criteria you're looking for, even if you state them outright in your profile.

All of this is part of the drill.

Online Dating Has a Dark Side

Most of the things I've mentioned so far aren't bad things, but simply things to keep in mind when dating online. However, online dating does have some cons. One of the cons is something

I alluded to earlier – that people tend to be pickier when dating online than when dating conventionally. A fellow blogger once said that online dating favors those who "look good on paper." He nailed it on the head. Because online dating means choosing people based on a picture or a profile, rather than based on feeling a connection or knowing who a person really is, people tend to seek out the "ideal" profile.

For example, research has shown that, online, men tend to seek younger and prettier girls than they would in real life, and women tend to seek taller and higher-earning men than they normally would. This fact is one of the biggest challenges when dating online.

Online, people tend to seek the ideal profile, rather than someone with potential.

Another con of dating online is that you will, from time to time, come into contact with women who are flaky, rude, or just strange. First, simply being exposed to so many woman increases the odds of meeting some weird ones. Second, odd or socially inept women will join online dating sites because they can hide their flaws much more easily than they can meeting people through more conventional methods.

Finally, as a guy, you may be contacted by fraudulent organizations looking to use your desire for women to get money from you.

Don't let these cons discourage you. All aspects of dating will have drawbacks. The more you recognize the drawbacks of dating online, the more you can work around them.

The purpose of this chapter is not to depress you or scare you away from dating online. It's to inform you of the challenges you are likely to encounter, and to show you that if you're experiencing any or all of these things, you're normal.

When faced with such challenges, a Problem Solver doesn't give up or complain about how lame online dating is. He may initially get frustrated, but then he adjusts his expectations and figures out what he can do differently. He knows that online dating is like any other skill – it can be practiced and mastered.

Adjusting your expectations is the first step in your online dating success. The following chapters discuss the next steps.

20) CREATING A GREAT PROFILE

One of the many challenges of online dating is attempting to attract women with only a photo and write-up of yourself. Because you haven't met in person yet, and don't have good old-fashioned chemistry to trigger a woman's interest in you, you must rely on a one-dimensional snapshot of yourself to stir a woman's interest. Doing so successfully is an art form, but an achievable one.

The psychology of attracting women online boils down to looking as interesting as possible on paper. This means that without your energy and personality to trigger her attraction in person, you must attempt to do so through your profile. A good profile includes flattering photos of yourself and a couple of well-written, descriptive paragraphs that show women who you are.

As part of my research as a dating expert, I will periodically log into online dating sites and read through people's profiles. Right away, I can tell which men tossed up a quick profile with a hastily written write-up and an old photo, and which men put thought into it. And the latter are much more likely to succeed. Thus, this chapter will outline how to create the kind of profile that attracts women. Follow these guidelines, and you will be far ahead of your online competition.

The Photo

When you check out women online, what's the first thing you look at? The main photo, right? This photo is not only the first thing you see, but it's probably what determines whether you bother reading her profile. Well, women are no different. If your photo sucks, you will get far fewer responses, which is not what you want. Below, I list guidelines to follow for your online photo.

These guidelines apply to your main headshot, the photo women will see first, unless stated otherwise.

- **Go for quality.** Your main photo should be high quality and flattering. It should look like you, but a flattering version of you. Avoid blurry or underexposed photos, or photos with red-eye. It's okay to have a family member or a friend take photos of you for online dating. I've done this for my friends and they've done it for me.

- **Variety is good.** Your primary photo will be a headshot, but you should also add a variety of other photos that showcase who you are. If you love to fish, let her see you in your gear by the river. If you ski, include a shot of you on skis. When you're doing what you love, you look happier and sexier. If you've traveled, include photos from interesting places and then talk about them in your write-up. Women like men who live interesting lives.

- **Look sexy.** OkCupid did some interesting research and found that women preferred photos where the men had serious expressions, especially if they didn't look right at the camera.[7] This gives off a strong and sexy vibe that women like.

- **No sunglasses.** The eyes are the most expressive part of our faces. To hide them is to hide yourself, and you will not get good response. This is true for your headshot; you can wear shades in other photos.

- **Wear color.** Color stimulates the emotions, so wear a shirt in a non-neutral color that flatters you. And avoid going shirtless – no matter how nice your body, women don't want to see that much skin yet.

- **No pets or kids.** These are fine for other photos, but not your main photo.

- **No photos with the ex cut out.** I am shocked at how many times I've seen this during my online research forays. Women will think you're too lazy to get recent photos of yourself. Also, the first thing a woman sees is your ex, even if it's just a hand or some hair. Don't do this. No excuses.

- **Keep it recent.** Avoid using any photo that is more than a year old. Otherwise, you won't look like you. You never want to fail to meet a woman's expectations by looking less good in person than you do online; it's better to look the same or slightly better in person.

The Write-Up

For most men, the write-up is the most difficult part of the online profile. This is understandable – trying to convey who you are in a paragraph, while sounding interesting, is very difficult. Fortunately, the write-up doesn't need to be long or poetic. But it does need to be well-written, descriptive, and interesting enough to spark a woman's interest. This section provides some tips on how to do that.

Watch Your Grammar and Spelling

Poor grammar and spelling will turn women off. Although more a reflection of writing skill than intelligence, people still harbor negative perceptions about poor grammar and spelling. So avoid them at all costs. You don't have to be a great writer, and the occasional typo or error isn't a big deal. But if writing or spelling isn't your strong suit, as with many men, have someone look over your write-up to make edits.

Be Specific

One of the biggest mistakes people make online is that they're too generic in the write-up. For example, you may state, "I love the outdoors" or, "I enjoy sports and movies." Most people like these things. Specifics not only make you sound more interesting, they show women who you really are.

Generic	Interesting and informative
"I enjoy the outdoors."	"I hike every weekend down at the lake." "I love walking my dog in Central Park at sunset."
"I love football."	"I'm a huge Broncos fan and never miss a game."
"I'm a big fan of action movies."	"My favorites are *Die Hard* and *Bourne Identity*."
"I enjoy traveling."	"Last year, I spent a month in Costa Rica." "My goal is to see the Grand Canyon someday."

See the difference? The phrases on the right are more interesting to read and say so much more about you. Why? They provide specific examples and paint a picture of what your life is like.

Show, Don't Tell

One of the best ways to craft a good profile is to show women who you are, rather than *tell* women who you are. Men find it very difficult to describe themselves in the write-up. Thus, the solution to this is… don't! Instead, *show* them what makes you *you* by sharing specifics about what you like and what you do. Some ways you can do this include: discuss what you do for a living, specific foods you love, hobbies you have, causes you're passionate about, children or pets you love, and how you spend your weekends or vacations. This is easier to do and tells so much more about you. It also sparks interest and attraction in women.

Avoid Negativity

While it's okay to state your preferences or where you stand on certain things, avoid knocking what you *don't* like. For example, if you're a diehard conservative, say so if you want, but don't knock liberals. If you're an atheist, don't criticize religion. If you're a carnivore, don't insult vegetarians. Having an opinion makes you look confident and attracts women who are compatible with you. Criticizing others gives off a "jerk" vibe, even if you aren't one.

Avoid Stating What You Don't Want

Always state what you like and want, NOT what you don't like or don't want. This is a very common mistake even seasoned online daters make. For example, men will state they "don't want drama" or "don't date BBWs." This is a major turnoff. A Problem Solver focuses on what he wants, not on what he doesn't want – if he gets an email from a woman who doesn't fit his criteria, he simply ignores it or sends a polite rejection.

Watch Out for Overused Phrases

If you ever look through other men's online profiles (and you should – you can learn a lot), there are certain phrases you will see over and over again. This, of course, means that women will see them over and over again.

For example, some men will express what a "regular guy" they are. They will use those words or something similar such as:

"I'm a simple guy"

"I'm a pretty laid back guy"

"I'm just the average Joe"

"I'm a pretty normal guy"

"I'm an easygoing guy"

"I'm a fun-loving guy"

"I'm a straightforward guy"

"I'm your average American male"

These statements are not only overused, which doesn't make you stand out, they're also generic and don't really tell women much about you. Instead, using the guidelines I stated above, avoid describing yourself and focus on describing what you enjoy in life.

Other overused statements include:

"Tired of the bar scene." It doesn't make you look good to tell women your primary way of picking up women was at bars. Men say this to justify why they're online, which is unnecessary. You're online for the same reason everyone else is: to meet someone.

"I don't want games." I've never met anyone, male or female, who wants "games." This statement tells women that you've had, and are probably still having, difficulties with women. That's not what you want to convey.

"Looking for my partner in crime." This is charming, but way overused. Same goes for "Looking for my better half."

Example

Here are actual quotes from men's online dating profiles, and why you should avoid them:

"I've been on this site over a year and haven't met one person."

(Seriously? This will only make women wonder what's wrong with you and avoid you.)

"I'm trying to figure out why I'm doing this."

(If you don't know why you're online, why should women bother with you?)

"I don't enjoy online dating."

(Yeah – women will line up to meet you, Mr. Positive!)

"I have a dog, and she will always be the most important thing in my life."

(Every woman's dream – to come in second place to a mutt.)

"Liars, cheaters, may not apply."

(Nobody wants a liar or a cheater. This advertises to women that you've been lied to and cheated on. Hello emotional baggage!)

"I'm a sarcastic guy."

(This is overused and says little about you. Remember: show, don't tell. Sarcastic can mean you have an acerbic sense of humor, which can be funny, or that you're a bitter, mean-spirited guy.)

If your not crazy and like having a good time hit me up to say hi!!

(Never state what you don't want, and watch your "your" vs. "you're." Also, "having a good time" can mean a lot of things. Too generic.)

Finally, you will want to avoid stating that you look or act younger than your age. This makes you sound insecure about your age, or just immature. Neither is sexy. Finally, NO WRITING IN ALL CAPS. THIS IS DIFFICULT TO READ.

Online Deception: Why We Do It (and Why It Doesn't Work)

While deception is part of dating, it is especially common in online dating. For example, some men exaggerate their height, some women lie about their age, and some people post photos that look better than they do in real life. Why do people do this? Deep down, we all want the same thing: to be liked and valued. People who lie or deceive lack confidence in themselves and believe, deep down, that no one will like them for who they really are.

This creates a lot of problems in dating. No one likes to be deceived; it makes them feel tricked and foolish. Then, they become far less trusting, even with people who haven't lied or been deceptive.

"But You Have To Lie to Play The Game!"

Many people admit that they deceive or lie because they believe it's the only way to survive dating online and get other singles to give them a chance. For example, a man may lie about his height or income online because he knows that many women look for these things. He rationalizes that once a woman sees how great he is, she will overlook the deception, or will be too attached to him by then to reject him. But it's more likely that will be the one and only date he ever gets with her.

Such deception may seem like something a Problem Solver would do, but it isn't. A Problem Solver doesn't lie online. Why? Because he's comfortable enough with who he is to reveal his true self to the world and accept that not all women will like it. If he has a "flaw," he learns to give it a positive spin and focus on his other great traits. In the end, women like confidence more than they like tall stature or high income.

Remember: dating will always make us hyperaware of our insecurities, and online dating is no exception. Facing those insecurities builds confidence.

Showing Your Best Self — Without Deception

Here are the most common ways men deceive online, and what to do about them.

Age. Lying about your age tells women that you're insecure about it. If you happen to look good for your age, you don't need to lie – women will see that in your photos or when you meet in person. Also, age won't be an issue if you seek women your age.

Height. While it's okay to "round up" on height (i.e. round up to 5'9" if you're 5'8½"), don't exaggerate your height beyond that. Trust me – women will immediately recognize your deception once you meet in person. If you aren't tall, make your profile great, play up your other qualities, and target shorter women.

Income. Don't answer the income question online. Your income is no woman's business until you get to know and trust her. Instead, emphasize your career and hobbies – an interesting life always trumps high income.

Your profile is the key to attracting women online. If you aren't finding what you're looking for, be a Problem Solver and search for ways to improve your profile. If you aren't sure, have some women look it over and give you some pointers.

Okay, now that you know how to create a profile that attracts women, you're ready to move on to finding the women you want!

21) SELECTING YOUR CRITERIA

One of the best things about online dating is it allows you to search for some of the criteria you're looking for in a woman. If you're into cycling, you can search for women who include cycling in their interests. If you hate smoking, you can rule out smokers. If you have a thing for Asian women, you can search based on ethnicity. The flexibility of many dating sites is one feature that draws people to date online.

When you create your online profile and start browsing for women, it's important to know what you're looking for. This means knowing what sort of relationship you want as well as what qualities you seek in women. The clearer you are on what you want and need, the more likely you are to find it.

However, selecting what you're looking for isn't as easy as it sounds.

The Biggest Problem with Online Dating

While having the ability to choose what you're looking for in a woman seems like a good thing, for many online daters this "good thing" winds up limiting them. Why is this?

When you look at the selection criteria on most dating sites, you will see items such as age, height, body type, hair and eye color, education, income, ethnicity, marital status, and religion. These items tell you a lot about a woman, but they tell you very little about whether or not she would be a good match for you. With all these options, many online daters choose their preferences based not on what they're *open to*, but on what they would *ideally want*. I call this "Design-Your-Ideal-Mate Syndrome."

Many online daters choose their preferences based not on what they're open to, but on what they would ideally want.

For example, despite the fact that you find a variety of physical traits attractive, you look for thin, white women with Bachelor's degrees because these are your "ideal" women. This greatly narrows the pool of women open to you and decreases your odds of finding what you really want.

Why do people fall prey to Design-Your-Ideal-Mate Syndrome? To some extent, it's the illusion of endless options I discussed in Chapter 19. When you have thousands of women to choose from, why not look for your ideal, right? But experienced online daters know that the illusion of all these options is just that… an illusion. The other reason people get picky with their criteria is that most online dating sites don't have the inclination or ability to let people search for the qualities that actually increase their odds of finding a good match – in other words, it's much tougher to search for the two C's. The exception to this includes match-based sites such as eHarmony or Chemistry.

I recommend you avoid the temptation to make the mistakes many others make when dating online; in other words, be less choosy with some criteria, and *more* choosy with others.

Criteria to be LESS Choosy About

When you date online, it can be challenging to find a woman you connect with. Thus, you don't want to limit your options by being overly choosy with traits that aren't important. Here are some criteria you should be *less* choosy about:

Age

The age criterion is the #1 way men reduce their odds of success online. How? By stating that they only want to date women younger than themselves. For example, if you're 40, you seek women 30-39. If you're 33, you seek women 23-32. This pattern, referred to as the "0 up, 10 down" approach – i.e. targeting women 0 years older and 10 years younger – is pervasive among men when they date online.

The problem with the "0 up, 10 down" approach is that it rules out a lot of women. Why? Because these men target women who are less likely to date them, and ignore women who are more likely to date them. During my online dating research, I found that while the majority of men were interested in women 10 (or even 15) years younger, the majority of women were not interested in men 10-15 years older. For example, many 40-year-old men sought women 28-39 or 30-39, but most women 28-30 did not seek men over 35-36. By contrast, most women who were 35-45 were interested in age-40 men.

By doing this, many men aim for women who aren't interested in them, and ignore women who are. Remember: in any type of dating, it's not enough to focus on the women you want – you need to also focus on who wants you. A Problem Solver knows he has far more options by targeting women who are more likely to go out with him.

It's not enough to focus on which women you want; you need to also focus on which women want YOU.

This doesn't mean you can't seek younger women or that you should narrow your age range. Instead, broaden your age range to include women your age and older. Some men argue that they aren't attracted to women their age or older. If you think women your age aren't attractive, then what does that say about your attractiveness?

I suggest you try a "10 down, 5 up" approach – i.e. if you're 40, seek women who are 30-45. This opens up a lot of options for you. Trust me – if you meet a woman who's 45, you won't even notice the 5-year difference. If, however, you're the adventurous type, I recommend you try "15 down, 10 up." You'll be amazed at the interesting women you meet!

Another pointer on age range: be cautious about seeking *much* younger women and women 18-23. The younger you seek, the more you come off like the guy looking for NSA or an ego-boost. If you truly want NSA, fine. If you want something more, expand your age range. Also, women under 24 are still developing who they are and should be off limits to men over 30.

Race/Ethnicity

In this day and age, more and more people date and/or marry someone of a different race or ethnicity. Some people feel that we should choose partners who are members of our ethnicity. This is often to ensure similar values or cultural beliefs, or to preserve one's culture or heritage. However, I suggest you avoid restricting yourself to any ethnicity when dating online. Instead, look for women who share your values and cultural beliefs, and who are willing to respect your desire to preserve your heritage. Often, this will be someone of your ethnic group – but not always.

For example, some white men have a difficult time imagining themselves dating a black woman. This can be due to perceived cultural differences as well as the way black women are portrayed in pop culture. However, not all black women are the same.

In addition, these days more and more people are of mixed ancestry. If you state you don't want to date black or Asian girls, you may come across a gorgeous biracial woman who you have a lot in common with... and ruin your chances with her. Why? Because she will see your preferences and assume you don't like an important part of who she is.

Any dating expert will tell you that you never know where you will find happiness. Therefore, don't rule out any ethnicity, no matter what your ideas are about that group. Keep this criterion open and see what comes your way.

Body type

In my opinion, "body type" is the most worthless criterion in online dating. The categories aren't very useful, and everyone's interpretation of "athletic" or "curvy" is different. Curvy may mean she has lots of curves but is normal weight, or it could mean she's overweight. Thus, don't waste your time limiting your searches based on body type. Go by her photos. True, photos aren't always accurate, but that's an unavoidable part of online dating.

Some men only search for thin women online. However, nearly all men are willing to date an "average" woman or a woman carrying a few extra pounds as long as they're attracted to her. Just as with age, you don't want to rule out potential women by being too restrictive. Broaden your criteria, see what comes your way, and *then* choose.

Other Criteria

Hair and eye color. Resist any temptation to make selections for hair color or eye color. No matter how great your love for blue eyes or your dislike for red hair, there is always an exception to the rule.

Religion. Unless it's a significant part of your life, don't make selections for religion. Religious differences are only a problem for people who are very active in their faith.

Education and income. Ignore these criteria as well. Fortunately, men aren't as choosy here as women are. However, I have seen a tendency for some men to rule out highly educated or high-earning women. This only makes you look threatened by successful women. I have a PhD, and every guy I've dated (all less educated than I) has been fine with it. What's important isn't a degree or an income – it's feeling like you're equals. That can only be established in person.

Height. While it's understandable you don't want to date a woman far taller than yourself, don't be restrictive with height. Keep a very broad range or skip this criterion altogether.

Many men grow frustrated with the lack of response or general lack of action they get dating online. A Complainer moans about this or gives up altogether. But the Problem Solver looks for solutions, one of which is to broaden his criteria up front. Give it a try and see what comes your way. Then, you can choose.

Criteria to be MORE Choosy About

As you can probably guess, I'm not a big fan of being too choosy online. It unnecessarily narrows your field of possible women and lowers your odds of success. However, there are some criteria you should absolutely be choosy about. This means sticking to them, no matter how hot she is or how bored you are. I list these criteria below, in order of most important to least important.

Type of relationship. Some sites allow you to indicate the type of relationship you want; on other sites, women may state what they're looking for in terms of casual dating, a relationship, or marriage. *Pay attention.* If she doesn't want what you do, don't even bother. Different relationship needs never, ever work. No exceptions.

Wants kids. Always pay close attention to whether a woman wants children. If she does, you had better too. If she's a maybe, you need to be a maybe. If she doesn't want them, then you can't either. Again, no exceptions. A difference in this crucial area is a deal-breaker that will end your connection anyway – so why not prevent future problems?

Smoking. Smokers don't usually belong with non-smokers. The non-smoker will hate the smell of smoke and/or nag the smoker, and the smoker will feel like he/she isn't accepted. There are exceptions to this, as some people can make this work. However, if it's important to you, don't ignore it.

Politics. People with similar political leanings do better together, often because our political views reflect our values and deepest beliefs. However, some couples with differing views do manage to make it work, as long as they share the same values. Be cautious with this one.

Location. While I would never recommend greatly narrowing the geographical area in which you are willing to date, dating women who live more than a couple hours away can have lots of challenges. Expand your search beyond these limits only if you live in a rural area, aren't having any luck, and/or are willing to potentially relocate.

When you date online, you'll want to focus on the criteria that matter most, and place less emphasis on criteria that aren't as crucial. Scan her criteria and make sure the important ones fit yours. Then, move on to reading her write-up. The rest you'll find out when you meet in person.

22) CONTACTING WOMEN

After you've browsed, searched, or received your matches on an online dating site, you'll need to attempt to make contact with women you find attractive and interesting. This is one way that online dating is easier than conventional dating – you don't have to make an in-person approach to a strange woman. Instead, you have the luxury of approaching her over email, and in an environment where doing so is expected.

3 Ways to Contact Women

There are three methods of contacting women online. I describe them below, and discuss the pros and cons of each.

Emailing

Emailing is the most common method of contacting women online. Here, you create a brief but original message and send it to her. In this email, you want to engage her in conversation and begin the process of getting to know one another. Details on crafting a good email are covered later in this chapter.

Winking

Most dating sites allow you to "wink," send a "hello," or otherwise let a woman know you're potentially interested without actually having to write to her. The pros of winking are that it's easy, it's subtle, and it allows a woman to know you're interested without having to face rejection. It's a way to get on her radar. Many times, if you wink, a woman will wink back or email you if she's interested.

However, some women don't like or respond to winks/hellos and consider them too indirect, preferring an actual email. Winking can also appear like you're just flirting, rather than actually interested. Thus, if you know you're interested in a woman, email her. If you aren't sure, or you don't quite fit her criteria, wink or say hello and see what happens.

Instant Messaging

Some dating sites have an Instant Messaging (IM) function. Everyone has a different opinion about this. Your best bet is to hold off on IM until you've established contact with her – i.e. once you know she's open to chatting with you. Otherwise, IM-ing a woman randomly can be intrusive and she may ignore you.

Crafting a Good Email

Your first email to a woman is important and says a lot about you. However, you don't need to spend a lot of time creating one – in fact, it should be brief. Your email should contain four things: a greeting, a sentence or two about what you liked in her profile or what you have in common, a request to chat, and a closing.

> *Example*
>
> Here is an example of an email you can send a woman you're interested in online.
>
> Hi Lawyer_Girl [**Greeting**],
>
> I saw that you spent some time in Brazil this year. I was there two years ago and loved it – spent most of my time in X, hiking in the jungle. [**Shows that you read her profile, and that you have something in common**]. If you're interested in chatting, shoot me an email. [**Request to chat**]
>
> Sincerely,
> Badass_Attorney [**Closing**]

Note how simple and brief this email is. Yet, it contains all four of the required ingredients. Don't skip any of these four things. It's poor manners to skip the greeting and closing (and all too common today). It's also unwise to not cite something from her profile that interested you, which suggests you're lazy or only interested in her photo. Finally, it's important to make it clear what you want, i.e. for her to contact you if she's interested. Also, if you want to increase your odds of getting a response, ask her an interesting question. For example, Badass Attorney could ask, "What was your favorite part about your Brazil trip?"

You don't want to put in more effort than this, as you will grow quickly tired of writing emails to women who don't respond.

When emailing online, cite something from her profile. Otherwise, you'll appear as if you didn't read it.

Other Guidelines for Emails

Here are a few other things to keep in mind when emailing women online:

Never copy and paste. While it can get tiring to construct emails to women who never reply, you never want to write a generic email that you send to all women. Women can spot copy-and-pastes easier than a chocolate stain on a white suit. Use my suggested template, and tailor it based on what you find notable or interesting about her. If you don't find her profile interesting, don't contact her.

Be polite. Sounds obvious, right? But good email manners are lacking these days, and men with good ones stand out. Always greet her by her name or "handle." Ask her questions about herself. Ask her how her day or weekend was. Also, many men tend to sound dull or uninterested over email, without meaning to. One way to counteract this is to include an occasional exclamation point or smiley face to convey enthusiasm in your written words.

Don't invite her out too soon. Don't ask a woman out in your first email. You haven't established rapport yet. You want to make sure she's interested in you (by replying to you and chatting), that she's polite in her emails, that she asks about you, and that she's prompt in her responses before you offer to meet with her. Emailing back and forth will give you an idea of what she's like. Have at least 2-3 email exchanges before you ask.

But don't wait too long, either. Avoid a common novice's mistake: the "email marathon." This is where two people build a friendship over email before they've ever met. People who do this are often not ready to actually date, and writing gives them a taste of dating without having to get out there. Moreover, if you do finally meet, you have a false sense of knowing one another well, which can change suddenly when you meet in person.

I learned this lesson from a guy who took forever to finally ask me out. In the meantime, he had taken a trip to Southeast Asia, from which he sent me long, descriptive emails of all he saw, like we were best friends. One we met in person, it was, by far, the most awkward date I have ever been on. We never spoke again.

Build rapport, suggest an outing, and if she doesn't go for it, simply cut off communication and move on. Online dating is for dating, not meeting chat buddies.

Never mention her looks. Mentioning her looks or complimenting her beauty sounds dopey or like you're only interested in her looks. Save it for when you get to know her.

Never make sexual or suggestive comments. Sexual comments or topics have no place in dating until you become more acquainted with her and you've established that she likes you too. They're inappropriate and will make her uncomfortable.

Example

Trisha joined a dating site that has a category for tattoos: one could select "visible tattoos," "strategically placed tattoo," or "no tattoos." Trisha had one tattoo on her hip, so she selected the middle one. One man emailed Trisha and said, "Hi there! I admit I am wondering about your 'strategically placed tattoo.' I can't help it – after all, I am a guy!"

Yes, being a "guy" might make you wonder about that tattoo. Nothing wrong with that. But mentioning that to a woman you've never met is inappropriate. Trisha was repulsed by this guy; and while it was her policy to reply to all emails, she ignored his.

What if She Doesn't Respond?

If you email women you're interested in, you may not hear back. This is because they aren't interested, have too many other options at the moment, or because you don't fit their criteria.

If you don't fit a woman's criteria, don't be surprised if she doesn't respond. This shows that you didn't bother to look at what she wants, or did but chose to ignore it. Not a good way to begin. Just as you have your criteria, women have theirs. If you fit hers, proceed. If you almost fit, what specific criteria are missing? If you're a year or two out of her age bracket or an inch or two shorter than her requirements, but you have other stuff in common, why not try? A Problem Solver might say, "I recognize I'm two years older than what you're looking for, but it seems like we have a few things in common, so let me know if you're interested."

If you don't fit her more important criteria, such as wanting kids, then don't waste your time. And, yes, you'll find that some women have ridiculous requirements, especially online. A Problem Solver doesn't concern himself with such women. He knows these women will learn the hard way that being too choosy won't get them anywhere.

However, if you do match her criteria but still don't get a response, don't let it get you down. It's disappointing, but it happens. A Problem Solver makes sure his profile and emails are up to snuff, and then moves on to the next girl. Overall, he may get frustrated that he isn't getting enough responses, but then he focuses on what he can do to change it.

Ending Communication Online

Sometimes, you'll be in contact with a woman (or several) and for some reason you don't want to meet her in person. Perhaps she doesn't interest you enough, or you see some Red Flags, or you've met a woman you're pretty interested in and things are going well. Since you haven't gone out with her yet, it's acceptable to stop responding. If, however, you feel that you've built a rapport with a woman and don't want to come off flaky, you can briefly mention you met someone and wish her luck. This will often be appreciated.

Much of your time dating online will be spent emailing women and replying to their emails. Getting efficient at this will take time and practice, but will be worth it when you get that email from the right girl.

23) THE FIRST DATE

If you meet a woman you like online, and she seems to like you, there will come a point when you'll need to meet face to face. However, the psychology of this first "date" is nothing like that of a conventional first date. Why is this?

In conventional dating, you meet a woman, talk with her, and get to know her a bit. You know what she looks like, you get a taste of her personality, you know you're interested in her, and you sense that she may be interested in you. Thus, the next logical step is to ask her out on a date. If she says yes, you have something to look forward to. You decide on a nice place to take her, pick her up, and take her out. There is no guarantee that the date will go well, but you know you have a decent chance of enjoying yourself because you've established mutual interest and built some rapport already.

None of this applies when you meet a woman online.

Instead, when you join an online dating site, you browse for women who look attractive (based on their photos), who appear interesting (based on their profile), and who seem polite (based on their emails). You agree to meet, but you don't pick her up – you don't know where she lives and she doesn't know if you're trustworthy yet. You don't spring for a nice dinner – that's a big outlay of cash for a virtual stranger. And, once you meet her in person, your online impression of her may be nothing like the real her – she may not look like her photos, or there is zero chemistry between you. Of course, it can work the other way as well: she may look so-so in her photos or seem only semi-interesting in her profile, and then you are pleasantly surprised when you meet her and she turns out to be awesome.

In other words, in conventional dating, when you go on a first date, you already know there's potential. In online dating, you go on a first date to see if there's potential. Thus, the first online date is a bit of an adventure and needs to be approached differently.

In conventional dating, when you go on a first date, you already know there's potential. In online dating, you go on a first date to see if there's potential.

The First Online Date is Not a Date

The mistake many online daters make is to treat the first online date like a real date. They try too hard, spend too much, or raise their expectations too high. Instead of doing this again and again and getting frustrated, a Problem Solver changes how he does things.

The first change to make is to realize that the first date with a woman you meet online is not a date – it's a meet-and-greet to determine whether you both want to go on a real date. Thinking this way works better for several reasons:

It reduces pressure. First dates can be really nerve-wracking. You want to impress her, you want her to like you, and you want to be your best self. This is all totally natural, even good. However, the odds of having mutual interest and attraction on a first online date are relatively slim. Knowing this, ironically, is freeing. You don't have to worry about rejection from someone you don't even know you like yet.

It reduces expectations. One of the biggest reasons for failure and frustration when dating online is unrealistic expectations. When you know the date isn't a date, but a meet-and-greet to determine whether the two C's are present, you won't feel as disappointed or frustrated when she turns out to be unattractive, odd, or just not your type.

Guidelines for the Meet-and-Greet

Of course, just because it's a meet-and-greet and not a real date doesn't mean you can slack off. Here are some guidelines to make the meet-and-greet as successful as possible:

Keep your expectations realistic. As I've said, the odds of making a strong connection with a woman you've only known online aren't great. Online dating is definitely a numbers game, and you have to go on a lot of meet-and-greets before you find one where the two C's are enough to warrant another date.

Stick to coffee or drinks. Because it's not a real date, you shouldn't have to waste your money or romantic efforts on a woman who may not even be your type. Meet for coffee, tea, or a drink. Lunch is okay too if you feel optimistic about her. Make sure you have an "out" if things aren't clicking – e.g. you have to get back to work, or you're meeting some friends later.

Be a gentleman. Just because it's a meet-and-greet doesn't mean you shouldn't be a gentleman. Some people get so burned out on disappointing meet-and-greets that they stop making an effort. This only makes things worse. When a woman arrives at your meeting place, stand up. Shake her hand and greet her. Get her a beer or drink, or at least flag down the waitress.

Example

MaryAnn met Jeffrey online and they decided to meet at a coffee house for their meet-and-greet. When MaryAnn arrived, she recognized Jeffrey, who was already seated at a table with his coffee in hand. When she approached Jeffrey and they greeted one another, Jeffrey just sat there. He greeted MaryAnn but did not stand up or shake her hand, and he continued to sit there while she got her own beverage.

MaryAnn looks the same in person as she does in her photos, so there were no surprises for Jeffrey. And even if Jeffrey was uninterested in MaryAnn, that's no excuse for being lazy or rude. Remember: who you are anywhere is who you are everywhere – a gentleman with good manners behaves that way with women he likes as well as women he isn't into.

Respect women's safety. I hear far too many stories of men offering to pick a woman they've never met up for a date or even asking her to come to his home. Remember, she has no way of knowing you're trustworthy yet, and there are well-known cases of men who have harmed women on the first date after meeting online. If she's too clueless to look out for herself, it's still wise for you to consider her safety. If the meet-and-greet ends after dark, offer to walk her to her car (you can mention your concern about the dark). She may say no, but at least you tried.

Make the best of a bad meet-and-greet. There will be times when you meet women who just aren't your type. This can get tiresome for online daters, and it can tempt them to start showing rude or lazy behaviors, like Jeffrey did in the example above. But why sit there passively, like a Complainer? Instead, use it to your advantage.

A Problem Solver makes the most of the meet-and-greet, even when he isn't interested. Maybe she's got interesting stories. Maybe she has the skinny on the best restaurants, hiking trails, or new bands. You can even compare notes on the trials and tribulations of online dating. Meet-and-greets are also opportunities to try new coffee shops, bars, or restaurants you've been curious about. Finally, each meet-and-greet allows you to learn something new about women, yourself, and dating. Trust me – this experience will pay off down the road.

When I dated online, I met a lot of men who weren't my type. But I made the most of every meet-and-greet, and viewed it as an adventure rather than a search for Mr. Right. From one Army man, I learned what it was like to serve in Iraq. From another, I heard all about his travels in North Africa and even got to see his pictures. From another guy who complained about online dating, his ex-wife, and everything else, I learned to recognize the signs of a Complainer with a crappy attitude!

If The Meet-and-Greet is Successful

Of course, if you keep trying, you will have successful meet-and-greets where you'll be interested in going on a real date. Sometimes, you'll know she wants to see you again. Other times, you won't be sure. Either way, if you want to see her again, you will need to ask her out. This can be done a couple of ways:

Ask her out at the end of the meet-and-greet. Once you wrap things up, you can ask if she'd like to meet up again. You can simply say, "Would you be up for doing this again?" or you can ask her to do something you'd both talked about on your meet-and-greet. As usual, look for a clear "Yes" or something similar. If you get a yes, let her know you'll contact her, and then do so within a couple of days. If she hedges or makes excuses, she may not be interested or isn't sure yet. Just say okay, shake her hand, and tell her it was nice meeting her.

Ask her out later. Alternatively, you can finish the meet-and-greet, shake her hand and tell her it was nice meeting her, then send a follow-up email within two days to ask her out. This method is more "mysterious," and a bit less risky, but still acceptable.

Either way, if you get a yes, you will want to try to set up something with her for the future. Schedule a date for the following week. If you schedule one too soon, you risk rushing things. Scheduling out too far – over a week – makes you look unavailable.

Overall, once you've braved the meet-and-greet and scheduled your first "real" date together, things are looking good! The online dating game has finally paid off! From there on out, simply follow the other dating guidelines I discuss in this book. You're still getting to know one another, so take your time, have fun, and be on the lookout for the two C's.

24) ONLINE RED FLAGS

Just as there are Red Flags in conventional dating, there are also online Red Flags. Many times, when I hear cringe-worthy online dating stories, I can spot at least one Red Flag that the storyteller missed. To some extent, online dating does mean interacting with strangers and does require some sense of adventure. However, while it's difficult to know much about a person from a photo and profile, there are certain signs that you should be on the lookout for. This chapter will discuss these signs.

Sexual Comments or Photos

While sexual innuendos, comments, topics are usually something I warn women to look out for – not men – such things are not a good sign coming from women either. Considering that online dating does involve interacting with strangers, and that some predators use online dating as a way to find victims, doesn't it seem strange that a woman would bring up sex or post overly enticing photos to men they don't even know?

Sexual comments or photos in a woman's profile are not a good sign.

While these women may appear sexually open, that's probably not the case. A woman who is truly sexually open is usually only "open" with the men she chooses to be with, not every strange man who checks out her profile or chats with her. Thus, when a woman telegraphs sex right up front, it's often a sign that she's troubled, manipulative, or in desperate need of attention or validation. Or, if she's young, it may be a sign she's naïve and hasn't learned that inappropriate comments or photos attract the wrong kind of attention. If you see or chat with women who seem sexual right off the bat, beware.

Bitchy Write-Ups

When researching women's online profiles, I have seen some seriously bitchy write-ups. These women will tell you, sometimes in great detail, who should NOT email them, who they WON'T go out with, or what they DON'T like. They may also mention their frustrations with online dating, with certain types of men, or with life. These women aren't feisty, outspoken, or tough. They're Complainers. And you can't please a Complainer.

Even if she contacts you first, or she's the hottest girl on Earth, or you still manage to meet her criteria and she seems to like you, don't go there. Her attitude stinks. As I've said, who you are anywhere is who you are everywhere. If she's that negative online, she'll be that negative with you.

Perfect Magazine-Style Photos

While it's crucial to put effort into a good, high quality online photo, even if that means hiring a professional, I urge you to be skeptical of photos that look like they're from a magazine. It is my suspicion that some of the profiles that use these photos are fake or fraudulent. Even those that aren't fake are still suspicious – a photo should represent a woman and what she really looks like. Even if she's a normal woman who just happened to use a glamour photo, be prepared that she may look different in real life.

She Looks Young in Her Photo

If a woman looks significantly younger in her photo than her stated age, or looks unusually good for her age, beware. She may be using a photo from her younger years, or a highly retouched photo. Remember, while some people look younger than their age, most people really don't. People who are 45, look 45, or close to it. If she looks young in her photo, that doesn't mean you shouldn't go out with her – if she's attractive in her photo, she'll probably be attractive in real life. Just expect that she'll look closer to her age when you meet her.

I know a woman who, after a recent divorce, started dating online. She used a 10-year-old photo of herself because it was a great photo of her. It looked just like her, only ten years younger. What was interesting is how many email responses she got from men, and how many of them were wowed by how good she looked, and told her so, even though they'd never met her. While her using such an old photo was completely deceptive (and wrong), it was surprising how many men were so easily deceived.

No matter how youthful she may look in her photo, go by her actual age, not the photo.

Flaky Behavior

If a woman is flaky when you email her or when you meet up with her, that isn't a good sign. Examples of flaky behavior include ceasing to respond to your emails, then suddenly responding later, then disappearing again; making plans with you for a specific night, then not following up when you try to confirm with her; planning to meet you at a specific time, then showing up late; making plans to see you, then cancelling them at the last minute. Of course, if she's sick or has an emergency, she may need to cancel, but then she will say so and apologize. But women who do the above things aren't women you want to go out with; not only are they showing insufficient interest, they also lack manners and don't respect other people's time.

Women who show flaky behavior online aren't worth your time.

And, unfortunately, some women may not show up to your meet-and-greet. This is extremely rude. However, a woman who doesn't have the guts to simply cancel the meeting, even over email, is a coward with terrible manners. Not worth your time, dude. By flaking out, she did you a favor by removing herself from your life.

Such flaky behavior can really bring out the Complainer in a man. However, the Problem Solver may vent a bit, but then he shifts his attitude. He knows a woman's flakiness reflects who she is, not who he is. Once he sees that a woman is flaky, regardless of the reason, he stops interacting with her and moves on to better territory.

Lack of Interest

With online dating, detecting a lack of interest is just as important as with conventional dating. It's harder to "read" a woman you hardly know, or haven't even met in person yet, but there are some signs to look for.

If a woman doesn't reply to your email or respond to your wink, hello, or IM, she isn't interested. For many, it's just easier to not respond than to respond to say, "Sorry, not interested."

Once you're in contact with a woman, look for polite, and reasonably prompt, replies. If she isn't that prompt, don't worry about it. Sometimes it takes time for two people to get to the meet-and-greet, especially if they're busy, dating others, or unsure if they're interested. It's how she behaves after the meet-and-greet that matters most. Then, look for returned phone calls and a clear yes to future dates.

Sometimes, a woman will agree to meet you and then cancel at the last minute. This is rarely a good sign, unless she has a good excuse, reschedules with you, and doesn't do it again.

With time and experience, you will learn to recognize signs that's something isn't "right" when dating online. Sometimes you'll learn the hard way. But no matter what, don't lash out at women who do the above things. A Problem Solver doesn't let other people determine his happiness level; he recognizes a bad situation when he sees it and moves on to something better. No matter what happens, these experiences will make you all the more savvy about women and dating, which will only benefit you in the future.

SUCCESS
AND REJECTION

25) REJECTION, PART ONE: BEING REJECTED

Let's face it: rejection sucks. You hate it, I hate it, and women hate it. It will never feel good. However, rejection is an unavoidable part of dating. No matter how great you are or how skilled your game, you will get rejected at some point. And while rejection feels bad, in many ways it's a good thing because it gives you information you can use.

The toughest thing about rejection is that we take it personally. Why? Because human beings take everything personally. But what does it mean to "take something personally?" After all, if a woman chooses some other dude over you, doesn't that mean you lacked something she wanted? Yeah, it does. But does that mean you're somehow deficient as a man?

No. *No it does not.*

Remember the two C's, chemistry and compatibility? These two things are what cause us to feel interest and attraction for someone. And if one or both of the two C's is missing, especially chemistry, we lose interest. Most importantly, we have no control over how much of the two C's we feel for someone. In other words, a woman cannot help if she doesn't feel interest in you. And if she can't help how she feels, why should you get upset about it?

We have no control over the level of chemistry or compatibility we feel for someone.

Rejection, in all its painful glory, can also give you some important information. It can tell you one of two things:

1) **That a woman isn't right for you.** If a woman rejects you, she probably didn't feel enough of the two C's with you. This means she isn't right for you. She didn't choose to prefer another guy over you, or to only like you as a friend. Looked at in this way, rejection, while unpleasant, is a good thing because it eliminates the wrong women from your life. The right woman will feel the two C's with you.

2) **That you need to work on your game.** If you find that you're getting a lot of "No" when you ask women out, or you're not getting callbacks from women, it's a message that some aspect of your skill set needs improving. In this sense, rejection is a great way to learn.

Many Ways to be Rejected

Here is a partial list of the ways you may have experienced rejection:

- She won't give you her number
- She turns you down for a date
- She doesn't return your calls/emails/texts
- She says she "just wants to be friends"
- She says she has a boyfriend or is seeing someone
- She says you're not her type
- She stands you up for a date
- She leaves you for another man
- She cheats on you

Chances are, you've experienced some of these types of rejection, perhaps many. And so has every other man. Fortunately, while you can't always avoid rejection, you can learn to handle it in an effective way.

How to Handle Rejection

If there's anything that separates the Problem Solvers from the Complainers, it's handling rejection. A Complainer takes rejection too personally, assuming it indicates some major deficiency on his part. A Problem Solver takes it less personally, knowing that his brand of Man isn't for every woman.

People sometimes ask me the best way to handle rejection. The answer is deceptively simple: say "no problem" and move on. Then, review the situation to see if you could have done something differently. If so, do that next time. Otherwise, keep looking for someone you share more of the two C's with. That's it.

There is only one way to handle rejection when you're dating: Say "no problem" and move on.

How you handle rejection says a lot about you. A Problem Solver may feel foolish or temporarily annoyed at rejection, but he does not behave badly. A Complainer, on the other hand, may do one of the following:

- **Give her the cold shoulder.** While it's okay to back off and keep your distance, being cold or unfriendly to a woman who has turned you down is a way of punishing her for her lack of interest.

- **Pester her.** Continuing to chase a woman who has turned you down is irritating and shows desperation on your part. Same with trying to persuade her to change her mind. If she changes her mind, she will let you know, but only if you back off and give her some space.

- **Tell her she should "take a risk" or "do something different."** This is another way of trying to persuade her, with the added dimension of trying to make her feel like she's boring and unadventurous if she doesn't say yes. Not cool. Let her decide on her own to take a chance on a guy like you. She might if you back off. If not, her loss.

- **Tell her she's not giving you (or guys like you) a chance.** Yet another form of trying to persuade, this time with a guilt trip. Never try to guilt a woman into dating you. This makes you look a child who wants his way, rather than a man who admires a woman.

- **Get angry.** While a man may feel a little angry when rejected, one who badmouths or insults a woman, or gets angry at her, essentially is saying, "Hey, you hurt my feelings and I'm going to get back at you for it." But it was never her intention to hurt you. She can't help if she isn't interested.

Why do Complainers do these things? Because a Complainer assumes rejection means that a woman thinks he's inadequate, and the above reactions are ways of rebelling against that belief. It's much like if someone said to you, "You suck!" and you respond, "Nuh uh! You suck and you're ugly too!"

The problem with this? The Complainer is blaming a woman for something that's HIS problem. As much as it feels like she's causing the Complainer to feel inadequate, she isn't. The feelings of inadequacy come from the Complainer himself. Take this example:

Example

Many years ago, there was a guy in my running group who I talked to sometimes. He'd offered to help me find a used bike, and so I gave him my email. Over email, he wrote several romantic things to me, then asked me to go skiing with him and some friends. I was honest with him, and told him I liked him but didn't feel I knew him well enough to go out with him, but perhaps sometime in the future. I was as kind as I could be.

He responded with a very long, multi-paragraph email about how "women always use the same excuses," that it was a "ski day with friends and not a candlelit dinner," that American women were "uptight" about hanging out with others, and how it would've been "different" if he'd been better looking.

I was taken aback by his angry email, especially since I'd tried so hard to be kind, but still honest. I never responded to him. He'd lost my respect.

Why did this man get angry? He took my lack of romantic interest in him, something I could not control, far too personally. He seemed to believe that by rejecting him I was somehow conveying that he was inadequate or not worth dating. In actuality, I thought he was attractive and cool, but I just wasn't interested in him.

Yes, when a woman rejects you, it may feel lousy and it may feel like she caused you to feel like a loser. But she didn't. On some level, you already felt that way about yourself, and her rejection simply triggered those feelings. Remember the famous Eleanor Roosevelt quote:

"No one can make you feel inferior without your consent."

A woman's rejection can't make you feel inadequate. Only you have that ability.

What if a woman told you that you were clinically insane? That's probably not what you want to hear, but would you get upset and defensive? Probably not. Why? Because you know, without a doubt, that you're not clinically insane. Thus, her criticism has no power. But because a man doesn't often know why he's rejected, he may assume the worst, that the things he's most insecure about are repellent to women he likes.

What if, for argument's sake, I had rejected Mr. Angry because I thought he was inadequate or unworthy? Is that his problem, or mine? Mine! If I thought he was unworthy, does that mean he is? No! His reaction to my rejection has little to do with my opinion, and everything to do with his own opinion of himself. If he believed he was the shiznit, he wouldn't care at all what I thought of him!

A Problem Solver may or may not feel badly about a rejection. But whatever his feeling, he knows it's about his own issues. He knows if he feels inadequate, it's time to do something about that.

What if Her Rejection Sucks?

Yes, unfortunately, some women don't do rejection right. They hem and haw, lie, disappear, or stand you up. How should you handle these women? Turn your back on them without reacting.

When a woman rejects you in an unkind or inappropriate way, it sucks. However, this behavior says a lot about her. It reflects who *she* is, *not* who you are. If you overreact to it, you let her bad behavior determine how you feel about yourself. As a shrink would say, you "give away your power." Don't do this. A Problem Solver may feel stung by a nasty rejection, but he knows deep down that any woman who treats him like that isn't worth being with anyway.

How to Reduce Rejection

No matter how charming you are or how ripped your abs, you will face rejection eventually. However, you can reduce the amount of rejection you face by following these tips:

First, Look For Signs of Interest

You have a lot better odds with women who make eye contact with you or smile at you than you do with women who look away or frown. This may seem obvious, but some men will try to engage an uninterested woman in conversation and then complain about how unfriendly or "bitchy" she is. You can still talk to a woman who isn't showing signs, but employ the Receptivity Test from Chapter 12 and recognize it's probably a long shot. Likewise, once you start dating, look for quickly returned calls and other signs of interest. Refer to Chapter 10 for details on detecting interest.

Then, Look For Signs of Disinterest

Once you make the approach, make the call, or go out on the date, keep your antennae out for signs of disinterest on her part. These include a disinterested expression, hemming and hawing about going on a date with you, cancelling dates, or taking too long to return calls. And remember the Mixed Messages Rule: pay the most attention to the messages that show disinterest. They're the bottom line.

If you're paying attention, you can often see when a woman's interest isn't what it ought to be. Then, you can jump ship before you get rejected, or at least see the rejection coming.

Wait to Make Your Move

Sometimes, men get eager and will make their move too soon, before a woman knows if she's interested. This leads to rejection. Instead, if you know that you'll see her again or have some way of staying in contact, take your time. Let the attraction grow. She'll wonder if you like her. By the time you ask, you're more likely to get a yes.

Also, waiting gives you a chance to assess her interest level over time. See if she continues to be friendly, if she talks about other men, if she mentions a boyfriend. All of this information can prevent rejection if you wait to obtain it.

Remember There are No Guarantees

If a woman shows signs of interest, that's good. But she could still have a boyfriend, only see you as a cool friend, or otherwise not give you the go ahead when you make your move. Back off, be a gentleman, and in some cases she'll wind up dating you if she ditches the other guy or changes her mind. And the fact that you had the guts to try shows her (and you) that you're confident in yourself. That never hurts.

Don't Target Women Unlikely to Date You

I want to encourage you to go after the kind of women you desire and to feel confident asking out beautiful and successful women. However, while it's important for you to aim for the women you like, it's just as important to aim for the *women who like you.* And while I never want you to think, "I'm not good enough for that woman," I do recommend you generally avoid women who are unlikely to date you.

For example, some men want gorgeous women or much younger women. However, studies have shown that most couples are similar in age and very similar in physical attractiveness. In other words, gorgeous women usually pick gorgeous men, and young women typically want men closer to their age. This doesn't mean you can't try for these women. It means that if you want to avoid unnecessary rejection, also aim for women who are similar to you in looks and age.

When dating online, pay close attention to a woman's write-up and to the criteria she's chosen. No matter how strange her requirements are, if you don't fit them, you won't get a response. You have a much better chance with women whose criteria you fit.

Ask Around

If you work with a woman who interests you or know people who know her, try to get the skinny on her. Does she have a boyfriend? Is she cool? Does she like men your age? These people may give you key information that could prevent rejection.

Yes, they may tell her you asked about her. But that can work in your favor. If she knows you're interested, she'll check you out, which increases your odds with her.

True, rejection is no fun. But it's part of dating. However, not only can you take steps to prevent rejection, you can also take a Problem Solver's stance toward rejection and remember that it's an opportunity to improve yourself. Learn from it and move on.

26) REJECTION, PART TWO: WHEN YOU'RE THE REJECTER

There will come a time when you have to reject women. This may be as simple as saying, "Thanks anyway," to a woman who emails you online, or not so simple like telling a woman you've dated several times and slept with that you're just not feeling it. Unfortunately, like being rejected, rejecting others is also an unavoidable part of dating.

Just as there is a good and bad way to handle being rejected, there is also a good and bad way to handle rejecting women. The more class you have as the rejecter, the better you'll handle rejection when it happens to you. Why is this? Because when you do rejection right, you will have better perspective when it's your turn.

As much as being rejected sucks, having to reject others isn't all that fun either. In fact, I would argue that rejecting someone can be just as painful as being rejected. It's just a different kind of pain. Many people deny this fact, but if it weren't true, people wouldn't try so hard to avoid doing it.

Good, Typical, and Bad Rejection

When it comes to rejecting women, there are three ways to do it: good, typical, and bad.

Good rejection. This is when a man rejects a woman in an honest and straightforward way. He might say, "I just see you as a friend" or, "I don't see this going anywhere" or, "I've met someone else." Depending on how well he knows the woman, he might say it in person, on the phone, or over e-mail. But he says it. Good rejection lets a woman know where she stands and leaves out any ambiguity. She knows it's over.

Most women appreciate a good rejection. They feel better about themselves and better about their rejecters (and men in general). Unfortunately, some women don't appreciate the gift of a good rejection, and use the opportunity to act out. If this happens to you, don't let it bring you down. These women are Complainers who take rejection as a sign of their own inferiority. Not your problem. Ignore it and move on.

Typical rejection. As you may guess from the name, typical rejection is the most common type of rejection. In a typical rejection scenario, a man rejects a woman without actually telling her. Maybe he just stops calling after a couple of dates, or doesn't respond if she contacts him. If he's known her a while, perhaps he begins to call or see her less, and doesn't admit he's lost interest until she confronts him. Or, in some cases, he uses excuses such as, "I want to focus on my work right now" or, "I'm still trying to figure out what I want."

Typical rejection is common online and during the first few dates, when two people don't know each other that well. But it can happen in relationships too. Sometimes a typical rejection is easier and less awkward for both parties; other times it is a poor choice.

Bad rejection. This is the worst kind of rejection. With bad rejection, a man treats a girl disrespectfully and/or behaves in a cowardly way. For example, some men will avoid rejecting a woman directly and instead will act like a jerk to her, hoping she gets fed up and leaves. Others will disappear without a word after getting involved with a woman, or stand her up.

Needless to say, bad rejection is a poor way to treat someone and is never acceptable.

Of course, women also can give good, typical, or bad rejections. The reason I didn't discuss this in the last chapter is that I want to focus on things that you can control. You can't control how she rejects you, but you can control how you respond to rejection, so the last chapter focused on that. Likewise, **you can also control** how you reject women, and your rejection style reflects who you are, so I focus on that in this chapter.

Unfortunately, many of us were taught that good rejection isn't the way to go, that being honest is too "hurtful." This is ridiculous. While *too much* honesty is hurtful, a straightforward and kind statement of one's plans to move on is less hurtful than disregarding someone, and far less hurtful than abandoning or treating someone poorly. The truth is, many people wuss out on a proper rejection *not* to avoid hurting the other person, but to spare *themselves* the difficult feelings that come with the job. But the more you avoid these uncomfortable feelings, the more they'll pay you back when you get rejected.

Good rejection takes guts and confidence, but it's much kinder and will make taking rejection easier down the road. Remember: rejection is a type of problem, and a Problem Solver solves the problem by facing it head on, not running away from it.

Rejection Guidelines

While a good rejection is preferable in many situations, there are times when a typical rejection is acceptable, even preferred. Here are some guidelines for how to reject women depending on the setting and how well you know her.

Emailing Online

When you get an email from or chat with a woman online, you may find you aren't interested or decide not to pursue it. The question is, tell her or just let it be? I've found that people are split on this topic, with about half feeling you should say something, and the other half feeling like it's better not to. You can say, "Thanks anyway, but I don't think we're a match. Good luck in your search," or that you met someone else. Or, you can simply not respond, with the knowledge that you're strangers and there's little need for awkward explanation at that stage. Personally, I prefer the former method and found that many men appreciated it. However, it's more work, so choose what's right for you.

Dates 1-3

The more dates you've had, the more a good rejection is warranted. However, typical rejection is still okay this early on. If you aren't interested in seeing her again, you can simply not call her again. This befuddles some women, but if they listen to any decent dating expert, they should know that no call = not interested. However, if you sense a woman is very interested in you or she contacts you, you're better off letting her know you don't think it's a match. This is more respectful than ignoring her. At this stage, you can do this over email if you prefer.

One of the more common complaints I get from women is when men "flake out." Examples of this include saying you'll call Monday and then not calling, or making plans for a date or activity and then never calling her again. A woman may hope you'll call Monday, but she won't expect you to if you don't say you will. Don't make promises you can't keep. If you find you made a promise and then changed your mind, that's okay, just email her and tell her you're moving on.

Dates 4+

Once you've gone out with a woman more than three times, this is generally considered "dating." It may not be serious, but some sort of "relationship" exists. You've gotten to know one another, and if she's gone out with you that many times, she likes you, period. Thus, if you change your mind about her, it's good etiquette to give her a good rejection and let her know you aren't interested. Never calling her again or avoiding her is hurtful and bad dating karma. A simple email will do. See the guidelines below for what to say.

After Sexual Contact

Once you've had sexual contact with a woman you're dating – and by "sexual contact" I mean anything beyond kissing – it's bad etiquette (and a bad rejection) to just blow her off if you've lost interest. If you've wondered why women can be difficult about when to have sex and insist on waiting and testing you, this is one reason – other men haven't done the right thing. She shared herself with you and you're rejecting her, so the least you can do is let her go respectfully. Do it over email if you have to, but do it.

Exclusive Relationship

Once you've established an exclusive relationship with a woman, it is never okay to end things by blowing her off or even emailing her. These are bad rejections. It must be done in person. Knowing she'll get upset is not an excuse, although I know it's hard to see a woman cry. The only exception to this is if she's nuts or you believe she'll make a scene – in these cases, do it over the phone.

What to Say

Okay, so now you know how to reject the women you date. But what's the best way to say what you need to say without saying the wrong thing? With rejecting, you want to deliver a mixture of truth and kindness.

For example, never tell a woman what you don't like about her. While truthful, this is unkind because, most of the time, what you don't like about her is about your personal taste, and some other guy may think she's awesome. The only exception is if she does something truly offensive, such as insult you, or she has a trait that few men like, such as drinking way too much. Then, if you want, you can tell her the truth, with the hope that she'll learn something.

In general, when delivering your rejection in person, over the phone, or over email, say something nice or complimentary, then deliver the truth. For example:

"I think you're great, but I just don't see us together long term."

"You're a cool girl, but I don't think we're a good match."

"I've enjoyed getting to know you, but I'm just not feeling it."

"You've got a lot going for you, but I just see you as a friend." (Only say this if you could actually see staying friends with her.)

"I think you're beautiful, but I'm not ready for a relationship." (Only use this if it's true. If it's not, use the above lines.)

"I enjoyed meeting you, but the way you talked down to the waiter made me uncomfortable."

These are honest, kind, and perfectly reasonable ways to reject a woman. Say them with kindness, but also with confidence. Again, if she busts your chops, challenges you, tries to get you to change your mind, or otherwise handles the rejection poorly, restate your point and then cut her off. You've done your duty and owe her nothing more.

It's Not About Her

One important thing to remember when rejecting a woman is that, most of the time, it isn't about her. You may not find her attractive, but some other man does. You may think her personality is abrasive, but another guy will like it. You may think she's uptight about sex, but another guy will prefer her conservative nature. My point is, remember the two C's – if you've lost interest, the two C's aren't there for you, freeing the both of you to find a better match. When you learn to view women you reject this way, you will find it *much* easier to handle being rejected.

Overall, rejecting women is something that no man enjoys. But the better you get at rejecting women who aren't right for you, the better you'll be at handling it when it's your turn.

SUCCESS
AND CASUAL SEX

27) A BETTER APPROACH

Ah, casual sex. Call it a one-night stand, No-Strings-Attached (NSA), or having a special "Fuck Buddy." Whatever you call it, this is when you want sex without the complications of a relationship. Most men may, at one time or another, desire casual sex. Many try to obtain it – some successfully, others not so successfully.

Numerous tomes have been written on how to get women into the sack. And while some have useful information, many of them push stupid, dishonest, or disrespectful tactics. Moreover, these books are written by men, most of whom have little more than their personal experiences to draw from. Something more is needed.

Clearly, NSA – and what's required to obtain it – is beyond the scope of this book. However, if you're in a phase of your life where NSA appeals to you, this chapter, as the final chapter of this book, will provide you with a few things to consider.

NSA: Is There Such Thing?

Sex is complicated. It's not complicated in terms of mechanics, but in its ramifications. And although an important purpose of sex is pleasure, another major purpose of sex is reproduction. A woman's sex drive is highest during the fertile phase of her cycle, which is also when she's most attractive to men. Sex and orgasm release many hormones that influence our emotions and can increase "bonding" between two people. And, as you know, sex can produce pregnancy, STDs, and other complications.

Given all of this, there is really no such thing as "No Strings Attached." To some extent, sex can never be truly casual.

Moreover, while a man may want NSA, that doesn't mean he's prepared to handle it. For example, how many times have you heard a story about a man who sleeps with a woman and then rushes to get away from her, or who insults her to his friends? Do such men seem comfortable with casual sex?

Likewise, take the man who goes out on five dates with a woman, has sex with her, and then when he loses interest in her, cannot manage to return her calls or deliver the proper rejection. If this man can't handle the awkwardness of calling or emailing a woman to tell her he's moved on, how can he possibly handle the honest communication required for NSA?

John Gray, the author of *Men are from Mars, Women are from Venus*, states that men may be prone to seek physical intimacy quickly, but that they often have difficulty with too much intimacy too soon. He says this best in *Mars and Venus on a Date:*

"A man's tendency to pull away is most extreme when he experiences intimacy before he is ready."

All of this may sound like I don't advocate NSA. I promise you: nothing could be further from the truth. I'm all for getting laid. Really.

What I'm NOT for is how most NSA-seekers go about it. There is often a lack of honesty, communication, and mutual respect with casual sex. Fortunately, there is a better way that can benefit both parties.

Women and NSA

Women often have a different view of NSA than men do. Here are some reasons why it's tough to get a woman to engage in NSA:

Women prefer relationships. As I discussed in Chapter 5, most of the time women seek relationships with men, not NSA. If you want NSA, you have to get skilled at finding those women who are open to it.

Women don't feel sexual attraction as quickly as men do. A man can look at a woman and decide, right then and there, that he wants sex with her. This is far less common in women. The average woman may admire a man physically, but she doesn't often develop sexual feelings until she gets to know him a little.

Women are more selective. Research studies have shown that, on average, women are far more choosy about who they will engage in NSA with than men are.[8] You have to be on top of your game.

In addition, there are numerous other considerations that will cause a woman to think twice before she even thinks about NSA:

Safety concerns. Often, a man may attempt to obtain NSA from a woman he hardly knows. This is not a big deal, as the odds of a woman harming him are pretty slim. Not the case for women, who must think about their safety when going home with a man.

Pregnancy. Any time a woman has sex, even with protection, there is a chance she could become pregnant. If she's in a relationship with her partner, even a casual one, she is far more likely to have someone to support her, whether it's to be there for her when she terminates the pregnancy, or to stick around and help her raise the child. If she has sex with a man she hardly knows, she's all alone. Having children is hard enough; raising them alone is terrifying. Every woman, on some level, knows this could happen to her if she sleeps with a guy she doesn't know.

Getting needs met. The only reason anyone – male or female – engages in casual sex is to get sexual needs met. But, as you know, it's often easy for a man to get sexual satisfaction, while a woman's satisfaction can be a bit more complex. No woman wants to agree to NSA, just to have a guy care more about his satisfaction than hers. Often, it's easier for a woman to wait until she knows a guy cares for her (and her sexual pleasure) before having sex with him.

Lack of discretion. Since women are less likely to sleep with a total stranger, if she wants NSA she must choose a man she knows or trusts. This means they may know some of the same people, and word could get out that she slept with him if he chooses to kiss and tell. Women may avoid NSA because they don't want to be judged or because they don't want others knowing about their private life. This is one reason why some women only engage in NSA when traveling.

The Double Standard. Moreover, some men still have a strong double standard about NSA. They want it, but think women are "slutty" for also wanting it. All women have heard men make snide comments about women who sleep with them on the first date or who are open about their sexuality. No woman wants to feel judged for her right to have sex.

As you can see, there are a lot of reasons a woman may not want NSA, or may not bother with it even if she does want it. By contrast, how many of the above concerns do men have to face?

Thus, if a man wants NSA, he needs to learn to assuage a woman's concerns. All of the above items provide clues as to how to do that. A Complainer gripes about how hard it is to get women to have casual sex. But a Problem Solver seeks to understand why, and then figures out what he can do differently.

Tips for Successful NSA

This section will discuss necessary steps to take if you want NSA with a woman. These suggestions are far from a comprehensive guide; rather, they are general principles that will help you handle NSA relationships successfully. Moreover, these suggestions are based not only on what women want, but on my interviews with men who have successfully navigated the world of NSA. By "successfully," I mean that these men get NSA with women who are not only willing, but who leave with good memories of the experience.

Know When You're Ready

Some men aren't ready for NSA. It isn't that they don't want it; it's that they aren't ready to handle the realities of it. Are you able to sit down and honestly tell a woman what you want? Do you feel prepared to follow up with her afterward, to make her feel comfortable? Do you have respect for your partner? If you take issue with anything I've discussed in this chapter, or if the advice in this chapter sounds like too much trouble to you, then you aren't ready for NSA.

Again, NSA is fun, but it isn't easy. Men who successfully handle NSA are not only willing to go that extra mile, they're more than happy to.

Build Attraction

Fundamentally, attracting a woman for NSA is no different than other types of dating. You still want to follow the magic formula from Chapters 6-7:

Success with Women = Masculinity + Respecting Women

Men who succeed in getting women to sleep with them attract them with their 101 traits, but make them feel comfortable with their 201 traits.

Build Rapport

You cannot talk to a woman for a short while and then ask her if she wants to come home with you. This will only work on very rare occasions. Typically, you have to spend time with a woman, get into some real conversations, and build trust, rapport, and sexual chemistry. This isn't because women are game-players who want to see if you'll do back flips for them before they agree to sex, like some Complainer men believe. It's because they need rapport-building to generate the comfort and attraction necessary for them to have sex. However, this rapport building doesn't take as long as you might think; for example, it can happen in one evening.

Read Her

While it can be tough to read a woman, once you've built rapport with her, you will want to assess her interest in you. If she's spent a lot of time talking with you, she's potentially interested. If she flirts, makes eye contact, or touches you, she's likely interested. And if she makes sexual comments or innuendos, she's probably interested in sex. There are no guarantees how she will respond to a request for sex, but if you've build rapport and she's showing strong signs of interest, she's more likely to at least consider your request.

Be Completely Honest

By "completely honest" I mean telling a woman, up front, that you're looking for NSA. I can already hear some of you say, "Are you insane? She'll slap me in the face!" Not if you build rapport with her first, and not if you say it the right way – with confidence and respect. The #1 mistake most men make when seeking NSA is to hide the truth. They hide it out of fear that they won't get what they want, out of shame for wanting only sex, and out of an inability to see things from a woman's point of view. Hiding the truth is yet another sign a man isn't ready for NSA.

If you play your cards right, you can be totally honest about what you want and get it. Women like to know where they stand (why do you think they hate when you don't call?). Only a coward lies; a Problem Solver tells the truth because he's comfortable with what he wants. If one woman says no, there will be another who will say yes. And it will be a much more enjoyable experience for both parties when the agenda is out in the open.

Make a Plan

Sexual experimenters and aficionados know that when you want to engage in a new sexual behavior with someone, you outline the plan – and the rules – right up front. Engaging in NSA with a woman falls into the "new sexual behavior" category. Once you establish she's up for it, work out a few details. For example, where will you go? What method of birth control and STD prevention will you use? What sort of acts are you interested in? Will you or she stay the night, or leave when you feel it's time? Will you exchange contact information, or not? This prevents surprises and failed expectations.

No Behaving Like You Want a Relationship

Another mistake men make when seeking NSA is to behave like they want more than NSA. Why do they do this? Because it's all they know. They take her out, call her all the time, share personal things, get the sex, and then wonder why a woman wants to pursue things further. If you want a woman to "get" that you only want sex, then don't blur the boundaries and do things a boyfriend would do. This doesn't mean being coldhearted; it means having boundaries, clear communication, and avoiding activities associated with love or friendship, such as long phone calls, spending time together outside of sex, etc. NSA should be fun and respectful, but not romantic or emotionally intimate.

What happened here? Toby did many things well: he stated his intentions right up front and he was respectful. However, Toby erred in one major way: he behaved like a man in a relationship. They spent far too much time together, shared a room, went out to dinner and explored the city together, and generally did things that a couple in love would do. As a result, Kristin ended up falling for Toby. Although it's always a risk that one person may get attached in an NSA situation, you reduce that risk by spending less time together and being less romantic.

Another no-no is the "Friends With Benefits" (FWB) scenario. If you want No Strings Attached, don't create "strings" by trying to have a second type of relationship with a woman (in this case, a friendship). You risk attachment and/or ruining the friendship. Research shows that when men and women are in an FWB situation, men tend to want to keep it that way, but women tend to want to either turn the FWB into a relationship or revert back to friendship only.[9] Remember: for NSA to succeed, both parties have to want NSA. No exceptions.

Be a Gentleman

Just because it's NSA doesn't mean you can't act like a gentleman. Unlike acting like a boyfriend, acting like a gentleman means making sure a woman is comfortable, that her sexual needs are met, that you walk her to her car (if at your place), that you offer her breakfast (if you agreed she'd stay the night), or that you say a proper goodbye (if at her place).

Use a Condom

Always, always, always use a condom. I don't care if you hate how they feel, if she's on the Pill, if she's a "nice" girl. Insist on it, even if she doesn't. No exceptions. Doing so lessens the complications and "strings" that come with sex – i.e. pregnancy, STDs, and 18 years of child support payments.

Be Discreet

If you want a woman to have sex with no strings and no drama, you have to be 100% discreet. This means telling no one you had sex with her. Yes, you can mention your liaison to your friends, but you can never reveal her identity, or reveal information that will allow others to figure out her identity. This won't be as much of an issue with a stranger you met at a bar in another city, but it's crucial when the woman is an acquaintance, friend of a friend, a coworker, or even a woman you met while out with your buddies. People love to gossip, and no woman wants to be gossiped about or judged for doing what she has every right to do. Discretion separates the masters of NSA from the amateurs.

Discretion separates the masters of NSA from the amateurs.

Follow Up

When you've had a sexual encounter with a woman, even if you don't plan on ever seeing her again, follow up to say you enjoyed yourself and to wish her well. You can do this as you go your separate ways, or afterward via a brief text or email. This says, "Hey, I appreciate your willingness to trust me and I respect you." Not following up says, "Hey, I got what I wanted and I'm done with you."

This brief chapter only scratches the surface on this fascinating and crucial topic. However, it should give you a few things to think about if you're interested in NSA. Remember: while you may seek NSA because it's what you want, men who truly succeed at NSA think just as much about what a woman wants. When it comes to casual sex, if a woman's happy, a man is too.

THE FINAL WORD

Dating is a great adventure. Like all adventures, dating has challenges, roadblocks, and other things that will test you. By choosing the mindset of a Problem Solver, you will conquer each of these tests by facing them head on rather than running away in fear. Problem Solvers don't know everything, nor are they always confident. However, they're willing to learn and build confidence through experience. And, eventually, they always succeed with women.

Enjoy your journey to success.

REFERENCES

[1] This is known as Confirmation Bias. See http://en.wikipedia.org/wiki/Confirmation_bias

[2] Sundie, JM, Kenrick, DT, Griskevicius, V, Tybur, JM, Vohs, KD, Beal, DJ. (2011). Peacocks, Porsches, and Thorstein Veblen: Conspicuous consumption as a sexual signaling system. Journal of Personality and Social Psychology, 100(4), 664-680.

[3] Pease, Allan and Barbara. The Definitive Book of Body Language. 2004. Bantam Books. New York.

[4] The "Human Performance Curve." See http://wikieducator.org/Introduction_to_Stress_Theory

[5] Lowndes, Leil. How to Be a People Magnet. 2001. McGraw Hill. New York.

[6] US Census Bureau, 2005-2007 American Community Survey

[7] http://blog.okcupid.com/index.php/the-4-big-myths-of-profile-pictures/

[8] http://www.sciencedaily.com/releases/2009/08/090811080749.htm

[9] Lehmiller, JJ, VanderDrift, LE, & Kelly, JR. (2011). Sex differences in approaching friends with benefits relationships. Journal of Sex Research, 48 (2-3), 275-84.

ABOUT THE AUTHOR

Dr. Christie Hartman is an internationally recognized dating expert, behavioral scientist, and author of five dating advice books. Her latest book – *Back in The Game: Succeeding With Women after a Divorce* – is a guide for men who want to shake off their divorces and find love again.

Christie has appeared on national television, including the Today Show and Fox News Live, and has made appearances on local TV shows such as News2 Denver, the Everyday show, and Daybreak. She's a frequent guest expert on the radio, has published articles for eHarmony, JDate, The Good Men Project, YourTango, *Denver Magazine*, and Cupid's Pulse, and has been quoted in articles for CNN, U.S. News, Match.com, *Chicago Tribune, Cosmopolitan, Men's Health, Women's Health,* Jezebel, Yahoo, and *Marie Claire.*

A graduate of the University of Colorado (CU), Christie earned her MA in Clinical Psychology, her PhD in Behavioral Genetics, and worked as a scientist at CU for 11 years. Living in Denver with her husband, Christie enjoys hiking and camping, and has a particular fondness for science fiction and natural health.

For more information about Christie's books and services, please visit her website at **www.christiehartman.com**.

INDEX

CPSIA information can be obtained at www.ICGtesting.com
Printed in the USA
LVOW04s1827110115

422398LV00031B/1307/P

9 780984 826216